LESSONS FROM
MY GUARDIAN ANGEL

Stories for Inspiration, Motivation and Meditation

Published & Manufactured in the United States by Cube17, Inc.

ISBN 978-1-945196-18-8

Editing and Design by Promocave.com
Cover Photography by Gustavo Mayoral

- First Edition -

www.LessonsFromMyGuardianAngel.com

To Christian Hoffmann:

My Mentor, My Friend, My Guardian Angel

Lessons From My Guardian Angel

Table of Contents

Introduction

It was one of my first big business meetings. I was wearing my good suit, actually, it was my only suit. My wife Gloria stood next to me as we took the elevator towards the last floor. The elevator stopped with a bell and we exited looking both ways. We saw the office numbers and turned right. The hallway was luxurious and we noticed the office doors as we passed them checking each number. The doors were double size heavy, wooden, beautiful doors that told you a lot about who works inside even before you entered.

"Wow," said Gloria, pointing at the oversized bouquet of fresh flowers in a large luxurious vase atop a hand-carved table, as we walked down the hall.

"I know," I told her. Her eyes opened wide.

We had plenty riding on this meeting. Our mortgage, our food, our livelihood, you know, the usual. This is why I brought my wife to the meeting. I wanted "the firm" to look larger than just me. Fake it until you make it! Or so they say. My wife wore a black business suit with a light blue shirt with my bottle cap and bottle opener cufflinks and a briefcase to top off the executive look.

Our potential client was an aristocratic Englishman. Or at least that's how he portrayed himself. He needed a consultant to help with his long term dream project of developing a high-end bottled water from the Himalayas. My wife didn't like to go with me to such meetings. She never did. We've worked together on and off since college, and sales meetings were not her cup of tea. Nevertheless, this was an important potential client for the family. So, after some deliberation she agreed to accompany me on this occasion.

"This is our door," I said. It was the last one on that floor. The famed corner office. Just thinking about how much he paid in rent made me cringe.

"A start-up and already spending eight thousand a month in rent?" I thought. "Not my style".
We were young. Very young. Not just in experience but also in age. We probably looked even younger, probably in our mid-twenties. I was hoping the suit and tie would make me look older and more professional. Hopefully even more expensive.

I grabbed the door handle with my left hand to open the door and Gloria grabbed my right arm, squeezing it tightly. I looked back to see what was wrong with her. Her mouth was dry and she couldn't verbalize her ideas. Her large eyes were glaring up at me with worry. I let go of the door handle and turned back towards Gloria grabbing her by the hand.

"You're sweating" I said surprised. Her hands watery with worry.

"You're not nervous?" she asked in surprise.

"Nervous?" I said as if I didn't really know the word. "Why would I be nervous?"

"For starters this is the most important meeting we've had for our business," she said. "We're not prepared, we don't have a presentation, don't know what he wants, who is this guy anyway?" she said all in one breath. "How can you not be nervous?" she asked again, with the expression on her face I know too well.

I bent down to leave my briefcase on the floor holding it between my legs, and grabbed both of her small damp hands while turning to face her.

"Oh, I see," I said just realizing she didn't know my secret. I smiled a slim smile and told her about my secret weapon. "You see, everywhere I go, everywhere I turn, especially when I go into these types of hard, difficult meetings, Christian stands behind me, towering over everyone, arms crossed, making sure I do OK."

Her large brown eyes melted into tears that immediately poured down her cheeks. I took out the handkerchief on my inside coat pocket and handed it over in one motion. Christian, our friend, mentor, and now Guardian Angel, had died recently.

Do You Choose Your Guardian Angel?

I've had my share of death in my life. Family, friends, many gone in their teens and twenties. Some of them made it to their thirties and a few even longer. My cousin Lachito died as a teenager, and so did my other cousin, Alfonso, drowning in a hotel pool during a vacation. My first experience with death came from my uncle Sabino dying at thirty years old leaving four children. Two of his own and two stepchildren. One year later his brother Arturo died leaving my cousins Arturo Jr. and Gabriel fatherless and my young aunt Clara devastated. It devastated my grandmother and completely changed her personality. I often ponder what happens after death. I've done so since I was a troubled teenager staring into the depths of the universe asking the tough questions teenagers ask, mixing them with hormones and a bit of confusion. I still ask those questions. I meditate on them, but the hormones are not there anymore!

I ask if my uncles Arturo and Sabino are in eternal happiness. Will I see my young cousins again? Will he be the same age as I remember him or will he just be the energy of my beautiful cousin Lachito? Will his hair be as black as I remember? His eyes as deep and his soul as innocent and confused? I think about my aunt Aurora who died so young. Younger than my age today. The doctors thought she had a cold and sent her home. She died the next day. Where is she now? I regret not having long conversations about life with her. I was too young. I never thought death would come again for those so young, those so good, those so needed.

I didn't choose my Guardian Angel. My Guardian Angel handpicked me. I don't know if any of my other family members guarded me before. I do remember seeing my uncle Sabino after he died. My mother told me last week I had the most pleasant conversation with him a week after he died. I made both her and my grandmother cry when I told them, "There he is, why are you crying?" I was five years old. I didn't think much of it as she told me the story. She, like me, is a storyteller after all, and reality mixes with fantasy. This happens not only on our paper, but also in our heads. This time however, the thought didn't escape me. I had the memory of my uncle there and my mother, his sister, crying. But I thought it was because of the death of her brother. No, her other brother, Arturo, died after, not before Sabino. Now I remember.

I thought about my uncle for a few days trying to retrieve the memory, and separate imagination and inspiration from history. It's difficult for me, as I tend to remember history as I want to remember it. I do remember my uncle speaking with me. I don't remember him after that. Maybe a presence a few times but not a permanent figure. It's an entirely different story after my good friend and mentor Christian died. The tall, tough German hangs around all the time.

Is he my Guardian Angel? Yes, he is. I don't know if he's my only one, I know for a fact he's not the only one I've had. I've had at least two guardian angels. Two that I can remember.

I know for many of my readers my religion will be very relevant to the text. My belief system and my education and background may seem relevant. It shouldn't. Sure, I will share with you all the information, but it's not relevant to the writing because these are very personal anecdotes, stories and feelings. I don't know if angels exist the way you want them to exist. I don't know if you have a Guardian Angel. But I do know I have mine, and we're on a first name basis!

Five thousand years ago, strange human like creatures appeared to the Son of man with wings spanning two meters on each side. Our ancestors of many faiths and many geographies called them gods, later they were called divinities or messengers between the world of the living and the world of the divine. Some of the earliest descriptions and paintings date back to the Sumerians, then the Egyptians 3,000 BC, and later the Greeks and the Romans. They've made their presence known in Hinduism, Christianity, Islam, Buddhism, Judaism, as well as many ancient theologies and mythologies.

Sumerians, Egyptians and Greeks all have images of angels. The most copied being the Greek images. These resemble normal Greek men and women dressed in the typical clothes of the time with wings, flying close to the ground, touching it with their toes as if to glide over the Earth. These Greek images seemed to be the inspiration for the more famous Catholic painters of the Middle Ages that produced the images of angels we're all familiar with. They largely consisted of children or large white figures with long hair and a white tunic radiating in light. It's important to note that these images where not originally created by these artists, they are replicated or inspired from previous art produced by the Greeks, Egyptians and Sumerians.

However, that's not what I see when I see angels. Not at all. Maybe that's why I'm a writer and not a painter!

An angel could mean something different to you than it does to me. It pushes different buttons, represents distinct emotions, theologies, and will raise different questions. This book is about a personal experience with such beings. An everyday experience not dating back five thousand years, not a religious encounter, but a life encounter with what I can only describe as a Guardian Angel. A being not alive as we know alive, and not a spirit as we think we know a spirit, but something else. Perhaps something of the imagination, or perhaps nothing greater than a simple Guardian Angel minding his post.

Do you have lessons or stories to share?
I would love to hear from you. Visit www.LessonsFromMyGuardianAngel.com and share your stories, read stories from others, and download special content and podcasts about the book.

PART I: THE OLD AND THE NEW

Did my Guardian Angel come from the old world or the new world? Was he or she here in the new world with my indigenous grandmother from the Pima tribe? Or did the Angel arrive from Spain by ship, crossing the entire Atlantic Ocean with my great grandfather Amadeo Garcia. He made the long trip accompanying his cousin Doña Ana to Mexico. Or did the Angel arrive from Scandinavia on the mind and spirit of my paternal great grandfather? Was the Guardian Angel of a religion or of a place? Of a culture or of a different time?

I am not sure where my Guardian Angel came from. What I do know for sure is that my great grandfather had one, maybe the same one I had as a child, maybe not. I also know that my mother had one of her own, or maybe we shared that one, hard to be sure as I'm not privileged to such things. Maybe you can help me figure it all out.

The Old World

My great grandfather Amadeo Garcia was born in Maello, a small town north of Madrid in the province of Avila, Spain. With a population of five hundred people, everyone was mostly related to each other by blood or by name. He got on a boat to The Americas accompanying his cousin Doña Ana as he didn't want her to travel the long voyage by herself. It was the eighteen hundreds, and Spain was not a good place for people like Amadeo Garcia with a strong mind and stronger opinion. This was a good excuse to leave the country, maybe for good.

Amadeo had enough money for the long ship voyage that would take him and his cousin as far as Cuba, but his final destination was the small town of Magdalena in state of Sonora in Mexico, a boat ride and long train ride to the north of Sonora. So, it was that Amadeo left his home, his mother and father, her brothers and sisters, cousins and friends to adventure to the other side of the world. It wasn't a difficult decision for him. "I have to accompany my cousin," he said as if there was no alternative.

Stuck in Cuba Amadeo worked in a factory by day and gambled by night, playing cards to accelerate his winnings and leave Cuba even sooner. His salary at the factory only financed his gambling. He knew with a standard wage he would never leave the island. He managed his money well. He paid rent and purchased food, the rest went into gambling, his other job. He was good at cards. He was good at everything, and his work-like approach at the game quickly yielded more money than they needed for day-to-day expenses. Amadeo was careful not to win big any one day and didn't play at the same locations more than once per week. He was equally cautious with his winnings, stashing his pesos in a secret hiding place he created inside his room. He purchased a hammer at the local store and very carefully removed the nails around a small piece of wood on the floor. He then placed the money inside socks and the socks inside rectangular tobacco tin cans. That wasn't enough for Amadeo, so he bored a hole in the dirt under his floor, deposited the cans and covered them with dirt.

That was his life in Cuba and every day Amadeo got up at four thirty in the morning, said good bye to Ana and I headed for a twelve-hour shift at the factory. This was his first industrial job ever. Amadeo had always been a cowboy and a farmer. Not like the cowboy you imagine, the ones from Sonora or Texas. He was an original cowboy, a real-life vaquero. His family were cattle ranchers before they even had cowboys in The Americas.

That night Amadeo was determined. He got ready to go out and look for a card game after a long day at the factory. The night was bright, illuminated by the moon, and hot. Not incredibly hot, but typical of a Cuban night. He walked out of his room and headed for the one place he knew he could win big, or lose big. This is where they conned foreigners from Spain and the USA. They had money, and they could bet big to later cheat their way into your pocket.

Amadeo strolled easily through the dirt road hands in his denim jacket looking up at the moon with his bright blue eyes. He entered the cantina and immediately spotted four men playing cards in the back. They seemed to know each other, laughing freely and slapping each other on the back like old friends. Amadeo walked the short way to the bar while eyeing the entire establishment before sitting down on an old squeaky wooden stool towards the end of the long bar.

"Rum," he told the bartender nodding. What else would you order in Cuba?

He looked around counting every door, window and exit in the mostly full cantina. The place smelled of tobacco and a cloud of thick smoke escaped through the large open windows like fog. It was loud with conversation of men blanketed by a feeling of trouble. Amadeo knew this had to be his last day in town. He needed to win enough money to make it all the way to Sonora. He already had a few pesos saved and was looking for a big payday.

The Spaniard picked up his glass and walked towards the table of card players. Amadeo was a thin wiry young man with yellow blond hair and cowboy blue jeans that matched his eyes. He stood out like a blond man in a Cuban cantina!

"May I sit down?" he asked politely in Spanish.

"Yes sir. We have a chair here just for you," said one of the card players smiling while pulling a chair from another table.

Amadeo sat down and prepared for a long night. He knew the cards where marked but didn't care. He learned to play cards in the old world, where sharks where much older, wiser, and had a bigger bite.

"New game new cards," Amadeo said looking each player in the eyes, his heavy Spanish accent giving away his nationality.

The hard men around the table glanced at each other. It reminded Amadeo of how a wolf signals the pack before jumping on their prey.

Amadeo felt confident in spite of the circumstances. He was a man of action, a valiant man who could remain brave at least five minutes longer than the rest. He decided to lose his first hand at cards, as well as his second. He lost the third hand but just barely. He was losing enough to let the others know it would be a good night.

"Tonight is not my night," Amadeo told the rest. "I'm usually very good at cards." He took an oversize drink out of his rum.

They all chuckled knowingly and shuffled the deck for the next game.

Amadeo drank heavily to complete the illusion of an easy target and waited with great patience until late at night to win four hands in a row. Big winning hands, the type of hands that would pay for a first-class ticket on the next ship, a train ticket, food, wine, and a bit left over for clothes and shoes. Maybe even a new hat.

"Finally I win one. You're not letting me win, are you?" said Amadeo seriously. "Are you setting me up so that I bet more?" he added.

After each winning hand Amadeo stashed his earnings in the oversize inner pocket of his jacket and pulled from there as needed for the next bet. This pocket was sewed in by his cousin Doña Ana specifically for this reason. Amadeo never kept his money on the table. That was part of his strategy, to never reveal how much money he came in with, or how much he was leaving with.

"I can't believe it. I win again," said Amadeo while finishing up his rum in one big gulp and ordering a fresh one. It appeared he stumbled into a winning streak. It was already past two in the morning and the crowded cantina was not so crowded anymore. It would empty out soon and Amadeo knew it. He placed his cards on the table face down. He still had a few pesos next to his cards plus a small pile he bet on his current hand.

"I'll be right back I'm going to the bathroom again," he said. "Please watch my money," he said to the table with a smirk, sticking his index finger out at the men.

In the bathroom, he took all his winnings out of his jacket and placed it under his hat making sure he had a snug fit. He then opened the bathroom window and with cat-like agility leaped out and started walking home, as if nothing unusual had happened. He was sure that would be the end of it. They would wait for a few minutes and then go look for him in the bathroom. By then he would be back home. Maybe even on a boat.

Amadeo took side streets and walked with stealth just in case he was being followed. As he rounded the next block he was surprised by two men hiding on the corner.

"Did you think it would be so easy?" they asked.

Amadeo looked around for the other two men. No sign of them. They were probably waiting around another corner guarding the other street.

"Give me the jacket," one said holding a knife in his right hand.

"You can have the money and the jacket," said Amadeo while taking off his jacket. Without another word or pause he threw the jacket into the face of the armed man while sucker punching the other with the entire weight of his body behind his strike. While the man dropped to the ground almost unconscious he delivered a quick uppercut to the solar plexus of the man blinded by the jacket. Amadeo looked around once and twice for signs of the other men and jumped into a full-on sprint.

This would not be the last time Amadeo faced death. It's not as if he looked for trouble, on the contrary, he was a man of unbendable principles, and maybe that's why trouble found him. It wasn't easy to do everything by the book, putting the law, ethics and morality before money and success.

Amadeo did make it to Sonora and started a family after marrying my great grandmother Josefa of the Pima tribe.

In Sonora, he hanged upside down from a tree, tied from the ankles by Yaqui Indians ready to skin him alive. He managed to stay alive because one of the Indians that joined the disturbance recognized him. "I know this man," he said. "He gives us coffee and sugar." Saved once again. Several years later he faced a shooting squad in the plaza in the early nineteen hundreds after the Mexican revolution. This time he broke the law. He threw a burning mattress into the municipal building and locked the mayor inside. They were corrupt and let people burn in a church a week before, so he wanted to spread the same medicine around. He was arrested and faced the firing squad the next morning. He was saved only a few minutes before he was executed by a letter from the governor brought forth by a writer galloping directly from the governor's office. Amadeo had saved the governor along with his family from an Indian raid years back, long before he was governor.

I'm not sure if Amadeo, my mother's mother's father, my great grandfather, brought these angels from the old world or if he found them here, in the new world. What is clear is that he managed to get into very particular problems in an irregular frequency. Problems and situations not as severe, but very similar to my problems, adventures and close encounters.

If my Guardian Angel came from the Old World it was most definitely brought by my great-grandfather Amadeo. An example of a man I only saw a few times as a kid. I got to know the man through my grandmother, one of my best friends, and all the stories she told me about him. Not two days could pass without her telling me an extraordinary adventure about her father, the man, the legend, the greatest man who ever lived. "He was the most handsome, the smartest, most hard working, and the most honest of them all," she used to tell me. I believed her!

Lessons From My Guardian Angel

The New World

Rosita lost the custody battle of her baby boy and had to give him up to his father. At least that's what the judge said. She didn't have many options. What could she do? She didn't have money for lawyers or long custody battles. So, she decided to do the only thing she knew she could do to keep her baby. She decided to run away and hide far away from her husband, the police, and the judge. A young beautiful woman only five feet tall with curly, kinky black hair, and an innocent manner that made you think she was a teenager. She wasn't, although she was too young for such things as custody battles and running away from the law.

This fairy tale marriage Rosita expected turned out to be a nightmare. She married an older man who promised she could finish her studies and travel the world. Instead she worked fourteen hours per day in the business while he traveled and spent the money on women, alcohol, and other worldly vices. After working and developing the language school into the most successful private school in the city, she didn't have a cent to her name. She had no time to see her mother and sisters, and traveling or studying was a long-lost dream.

He only gave Rosita enough for the bus ride to and from school. She was way too young and naive to take money for her own from the business. She didn't know by law it was also her business, and he had her scared for her life. She worked while he bought a new plane, had new girlfriends, and spent her hard earned money while keeping tight control over her life. The fairy tale dream turned into a nightmare broken only by a surprise. She didn't want to, but she was now pregnant.

"No, I can't be," she thought. "I can't be pregnant. What will he do to this child? I can't let anything happen to this baby." She cried herself to sleep every night.

Days turned into weeks and her baby grew inside her. She was radiant with a soft glow that emanated from her heart and illuminated a room. She didn't slowdown the first few months, but the doctor told her she couldn't work fourteen hour days. She decided to turn her life inside out. Rosita would do the best thing for the baby. She rubbed her big belly thinking "I will leave him; I don't want this for my child." It was one thing to stay in an abusive relationship, another to bring a new protagonist to the story.

Rosita prepared to file for a divorce and to put an end to this. She never thought he would deny it. "How dare you think you can leave me?" he told her.

He denied the divorce and the case went to court in the municipality of Tijuana, Baja California, Mexico. Rosita's husband knew he had no chance of winning custody and she did too. The father never gets the child and he was a foreigner, an American living in Mexico. But he was as smart as he was cunning and he gave such a large sum of cash to bribe the judge that custody was granted to the father.

This, however was not her first heartbreak and it wouldn't be her last. Rosita's first heartbreak was just as large and twice as bad. It happened one afternoon when she walked home from school as a twelve-year-old girl to find all her clothes piled on the sidewalk. Her mother arguing with the men ransacking the house and throwing it all on the street. They lost the house. The only thing they'd ever had. Where would she live with her five siblings and her mother? Her mother was victim to a smart, cunning man herself. The first man Rosita ever loved. Her father was very loving and kind to her, he told her he loved her, and she loved him. Until one day he just left and never came back. He abandoned her, her five siblings and her mother. Rosita's mother was left to feed her six children, three boys and three girls. She worked selling business cards and other printing services door to door visiting every business along the main boulevard in Tijuana.

Rosita suffered the consequences as much as her mother. Not only emotional consequences but those of life. As the oldest girl of the family she had to drop out of school and get a job to help support the family. She had to leave the one thing, the only thing she loved more than anything in the world, learning. So, it was, she left junior high for clerical school and become a secretary. She thought her luck changed when he met her American husband a few years later. Finally, she could go back to school, have nice things, read as much as she wanted and help her family. Maybe even move to the USA and work on her English. The true story was not the story she imagined.

After an official family meeting, they decided together the best thing for her was to go away and hide. "We don't know what he's capable of," said her sister.

"We'll go to Mexico City," her brother told her. "I will go with you and we'll stay there as long as we need to." Her brother Pepe was very protective of his older sister.

At least Rosita had her family, her mother, sisters and brothers. They would not let her do this on her own, his brother would go with her to the largest city in the world. And so it was, Rosita and her brother Pepe disappeared that night with the boy now two years old headed for Mexico City. They decided to look for their estranged father. Maybe he could help them find a job, this was the least he could do after not sending a cent to the family all these years.

Mexico City was better than they ever imagined. Their father got them both a job at his large company printing school books for the entire Mexican public school system. This was a very lucrative government contract that printed books for every single student in Mexico, from first to sixth grade. The contract was an incredible business opportunity. "As good as printing money," Rosita's father told her repeatedly. And he had some experience doing that. He did some time for printing US dollar bills back when he worked for the FBI. But that's another story!

Rosita's life was changing for the better. She had a good paying job and a beautiful apartment provided by a government official free of charge, and she worked and lived with her brother. It looked like her father was paying his dues and her future looked brighter. Salary was great, benefits were full, and she could even send money back home to her mother. Now she needed to focus on the custody problem. She knew if she ever went back she could lose her baby.

Rosita worked as a bookkeeper and administrator, handling all the money from the business, making deposits, paying suppliers and processing payroll. Her brother Pepe worked as a printer, a trade he learned at home and practiced since he was a teenager. There was a lot of work and a lot of money.

One day Rosita was working in her office overlooking the massive print shop when her father walked in with haste. She turned to face him and before she could greet him he interrupted.

"Here is the check for the next run of books," he said as he handed her a plain white envelope.

"Don't deposit the check," he said looking her straight in the eye. "I want you to leave the office right now and take nothing with you but your purse, go cash the check, and go home."

She tried to interject with a question but he stopped her holding his hand up in a stop motion.

"Listen to me," he said. "Go home and pack tonight and move out. There is enough money here to last you a year". He was in a hurry, glancing nervously behind his back as he spoke.

"Whatever is wrong I can help fix it," she said.

He smiled a gentle smile and stopped himself for just a second. A smile that acknowledged her innocence. "Rosita, please do as I tell you," he leaned down and whispered. He then kissed her forehead and left never to be seen or heard from again.

Rosita did not do as her father said. She was the manager, the boss, she could fix whatever problem her father had in the business. So she deposited the check and went home. The next morning she showed up for work like any other day. As soon as she entered the building it was invaded by teamsters and union representatives.

"We're taking over the business and the equipment," a man in a suit said while handing her an official looking letter.

"You can't do this," said Rosita. "Let me speak with your boss!" she demanded.
One of the employees, a friend of hers, came up and whispered in her ear "You should go before they hurt you, these are bad man sent by the new government to take over."

Rosita left the building crying looking for her brother. After she found him and explained what happened they went back to the apartment to try and contact their father. As they approached the door they saw two small trash bags outside the door with a note that read:

Dear Rosita:

You can take this bag I packed for you. Leave now.
If you try to go into the apartment, I'll call the police and have you arrested.

Thank You,

El Coronel

"Let's go right now," Rosita told her brother.
"But our things are still in there, he can't get away with this," he said.
"We have to go now," she said, "He can really have us arrested, he's in the army."

Once again, like as a young girl, Rosita was homeless because of her father. The trio, the two siblings and the young child all walked with their trash bags full of clothes to the nearest payphone to see if they could reach their father. She called his home "He moved out yesterday," they told her. She looked to his brother tears in her eyes not knowing what was happening. The three of them where homeless, their bank accounts frozen, afraid, standing in the middle of Mexico City.

"Why are you crying?" asked her baby boy. She wiped her tears as best she could and tried to get her feelings out of the way allowing the problem solving part of the brain to take over. She looked to her brother in surprise as she remembered something.

"The business card," she said.

"What? What business card?" asked Pepe.

She quickly dove into her purse to find the business card.

"If you're ever in trouble you call this man. He will help you. It doesn't matter what the problem is, he will help you," Rosita's father once told her.

She looked at the business card, it was a candy company. "Is this another one of my father's stories?" she thought. But she didn't have anything to lose, so she unhooked the telephone and dialed zero.

"Operator, I would like to make a collect call," said Rosita. She gave the name and number and the phone rang five times.

"This is the office of Mr. Rafael, how can I help you?" a female voice answered.

"I have a collect call for Mr. Rafael from Miss Rosa Sandoval," said the operator.

"This is an office," said the voice on the other side.

Rosita interrupted "Hello my father is Horacio Sandoval and he told me to call this number if I was ever in trouble," she said as quickly as she could before they even thought of disconnecting the call.

"I'm sorry Mr. Rafael is busy he doesn't take unscheduled calls. If you would like to leave a message…"

"Listen to me," Rosita interrupted with anger, desperation and courage. "Tell Rafael Rosa Sandoval, Horacio's daughter, is on the phone and let him make the decision. If you don't he'll be very angry." She said with a voice and heaviness she never ever used before.

"Oh, let me see, one moment," said the female voice.

Rosita waited looking at his brother nodding yes. He too was nervous and swallowed hard.

After only a few seconds somebody came to the phone.
"I'll accept the call".
Rosita started crying. It seemed a small victory, but she needed something to grab on to, whatever that was.

"Rosita, how are you? This is Rafael," said a kind voice.

"I am fine, I'm the daughter of," she continued but was cut off.

"I know who you are," said the man. "What can I do for you?" he asked.

Rosita started explaining but a few seconds in he interrupted again.

"You said you're on the street with no place to stay?" he asked to clarify.

"Yes, my brother and my son are with me," she said.

"I will send my driver right away," he said.

Rosita sighed in relief, not only because of the call, but because she didn't have money for a taxi to go see him.

After a short conversation Rosita hung up the phone and recited the entire call to her brother. He listened intently hoping for a happy ending the entire time.

"You wait for me here with him," she said trying not to make a big deal of it so that her baby boy would not notice what was happening.

"I don't know this man so I don't want to take you until I know it's safe," she said.
Pepe reluctantly agreed to stay behind. She was older after all, and you obey your older sister.

When she got there Rafael and his wife were waiting for her outside on the parking lot. It was a big factory, one of the largest candy companies in the entire country.

"Rosita how are you?" they asked.

She was confused. She didn't know these people. They entered the building and immediately she smelled sweetness. She inhaled deeply.

"Ah that smells great," she exclaimed.

"Oh yes, it smells like candy all year long. You always feel like a kid around here," said Rafael.

They continued walking and climbed stairs to Rafael's office. As they entered the large fancy corner office she figured out he was either the owner or the manager of the company. He had the largest office she's ever seen with a secretary parked outside his door.

"Your father can never stop talking about you," he told her. "Please sit down." There was a small living room inside the office with several leather couches. They all sat. The secretary came in with a tray of cups, coffee, and a pitcher of water and placed it on the coffee table between them. Rafael poured Rosita a cup without asking. He then proceeded to tell her an incredible story, more incredible than her own, more incredible than any story she ever heard.

"I was an orphan living in one of the local state run orphanages when you're father found me," he started the tale. "I used to sneak out to beg for money or food as we didn't have enough in the home. I cleaned windshields in the city or begged between the cars on a stop light. There is where your father found me," he said.

Rosita had her mouth open. She looked around the luxurious office, the large well-manicured man and his beautifully dressed wife that seemed she had recently jumped out of a Vogue magazine. "How can this be?" she thought, but maintained silence to hear the story.

"Your father saw me a couple of times while driving through my stoplight and started speaking with me, asking me questions about where I lived and what I ate. He found out I was an orphan and ended up taking care of me. He gave me food, shelter, an education."

Rosita looked at him befuddled. The man who left six children and a wife picked up a stranger out of the street and became a father to him, it just didn't make any sense. To this man her father Horacio was a hero. To her she was, well, not. He continued with the story but his wife interrupted.

"Where's your son and your brother?" she asked.

"They're back outside the apartment," said Rosita.

"Let's continue this conversation at the house," she said, "You're staying with us, all of you." Before she could protest, ask questions or weigh her options, Rosita realized she didn't have anywhere else to go. Her boy was probably hungry, maybe cold, definitely confused. Her brother worried sick about her leaving by herself.

"Can we go get them?" asked Rosita, hoping for a yes.

Rafael pushed a button and talked to the intercom "Have the driver ready, we're leaving."
Rosita stood up and Rafael's wife gave her a hug.

"Poor girl, you're going to be alright now. You're with us," she told her.

Rosita held back her tears. She still needed to pick up her brother and son.

When Rosita entered Rafael's house she was greeted by two servants and the cook. This is a mansion, she thought looking at her brother.

He looked around in wonder at the large doors, the furniture, and the decorations. Indeed, they had a lot of money, servants, a driver and a mansion, not to mention one of the best well known candy companies in the country.

A one night stay turned into two, then three, then Rosita moved into the guest house inside the property. Pepe left for Tijuana a few days after to help his mother. Rafael helped Rosita find a great job as the assistant to a high-level government official in the treasury. After a few months, she moved out of the guest house closer to her work in the city in the famous district of La Condesa only three miles from the Zócalo, the main square in the largest city in the world at the time. There Rosita and her child, now three years old, lived with Mrs. Flor, an elderly woman who had an extra room to rent.

Lost

Rosita arranged for a babysitter to pick up her son at the day care facility five blocks away, and bring him to the apartment and play with him until she came back from work. She was to stay inside the house with the boy at all times and never go outside, not even to the park. Mexico City was a large and dangerous city and a boy wouldn't last five minutes in the middle of the city.

That day the babysitter decided she would go see her boyfriend at the tortillería a few blocks away. She took the small three-year-old boy at her charge disobeying, Rosita's orders.

"I'll only go say hello to my boyfriend and be back in ten minutes," she thought.

The young woman and the boy walked a few blocks to the tortilla store where she locked eyes with a young man and talked for what seemed an eternity to the young boy.

"Let's go back," the boy told her. He spoke as a boy twice his age.

"Wait here," she said standing out on the street.

The boy started looking at birds, cars passing, people walking, tortillas flying off the machine, becoming bored and irritated with the boring trip.

"It's time to go back," he insisted.

She completely ignored the boy. He persisted with no luck. He took a few steps back and looked to one way and the other to figure out where they came from.

"That way," he said to himself and started walking with his tiny short legs.

He took no more than twenty paces when he was absorbed by the large crowd of the city. Imagine a city twice as large as New York, where it seemed to the boy they were all out walking that day. He waited for a green light to cross the street and surfed the wave of people to the other side. The boy walked another long block.

"This is very far," the boy thought. "Much further than I remember," but he kept walking between the legs of all the grownups walking in a hurried pace.

The boy grew tired of walking in his small sandals. He also wore tiny khakis and a vertical striped shirt. His little fit heart from walking. He turned to the left and to the right. He could only see legs. He looked up to see people flying by in both directions. He walked to the end of the sidewalk and didn't recognize any landmarks.
"I'm lost."

He continued walking another long block all the way to the pedestrian crossing. In the middle of the street parked on the middle sidewalk was a police car with a driver inside. Outside he saw a policeman directing traffic. A car passed inches from the sidewalk and he jumped back scared.
"How can I get to that man?" he thought.

As the signal light turned green he jumped into the street in front of everyone before the multitude whisked him to the other side, and when he was in the middle of the street turned to the left running to the man in uniform. The man was talking with his partner with his back to the boy. The boy looked up at him as if looking at a giant. He pulled his pant leg and took a quick step back with his hands behind his back. The police officer turned to look back and then look down at the boy.

"My name is Jorge and I'm lost," he said.

The tall man looked at the small child. "He can talk," he thought. He looked both ways looking for parent and saw none.

"What did you say?" the man said looking down at the boy.

"My name is Jorge and I'm lost," he repeated.

"You're lost?" he asked.

"Yes, that's what I said," he retorted.

The man took his police hat off and scratched his head. He looked back at his partner. "He's lost," he told him, chuckling.

"Where's your mother?" he asked putting his hand on his knees to lean down.
"She's working but she'll come home soon," he answered.
"Did you get out of the house?" he asked.
"No, the babysitter took me for a walk and I got lost," Jorge answered.
The tall policeman looked back to his partner again not believing how much this kid can talk.
"He's like a midget," he told his partner.

"I'm not afraid," the boy told the officer. "I know where I live, but I can't find it."

"Oh I see, so where do you live?" he asked.

"I live in front of the dragon," the boy said.

The man looked back again. His partner shrugged.

"Why are you parked on the sidewalk?" Jorge asked.

The man bellowed a laugh. "I told you not to park on the sidewalk," he told his partner.

He placed his hand on the small boy's head and gave it a little shake. "You and I are going to be really good friends," he said.

A few blocks away the babysitter looked back and did not see the boy. "Where's the boy?" she asked. She looked around "Where's the boy?!" she screamed. She walked a few paces to the right and a few paces to the left. The boy was gone. She cried all the way back to the apartment.

"Mrs. Flor, I lost the boy," she told the old woman.

"What do you mean you lost the boy?" Flor answered confused.

"Yes, I lost him. I lost him!" she covered her face with her hands and wept.

"But where did you lose him? He must me around here or maybe outside," Flor said.

"You don't understand, I just went out for ten minutes and I lost him," she said.

"You went out? What do you mean you went out, you know you're not supposed to go out?" Flor said angrily.

"It was just for a moment. I don't know what happened. One moment he was there and then he was gone!" she confessed.
Flor went for the phone and dialed it. "Rosita, are you sitting down?"

Rosita almost fainted. She had to get her legs back before leaving work in a taxi. Panic, fear, anger, all came down to her stomach at the same time. She wanted to throw up. She rushed home and got the story as best she could. She called the police and rushed out looking for her boy.

Jorge was in the back of the police car driving around the city with ice cream all over his face and a lollipop on his hand.

"Do you recognize anything?" asked the officer.

"No, all the buildings look the same," the boy said.

The two men chuckled. "This kid is funny," one said, and they kept on driving.

The officers reported the boy to dispatch, but the mother had reported it to another police station, the one for emergencies, and as the boy was not at the police station, they never filed a "lost child" report. The mother never knew he was safe.

"I live in the building in front of the dragon," the boy said again.

The two officers looked at each other. There wasn't any dragon in La Condesa.
"Tell me about the dragon," Jorge's new friend asked. "Is it a photo or a painting? How big is the dragon?" he asked, turning back on his seat to look at the boy.

"No, it's a game. I climb the dragon and play," said the boy.

The two men looked at each other thinking.

"Are you talking about the playground in the park?" asked Jorge's friend.

"Yes, the dragon in the park. You can climb it, you can also get on the swings and the other games," said Jorge.

"Oh my God, I know where that is," said the tall policeman. He gave directions to the officer and they drove to a park.

Little Jorge got out of the patrol car with his new friend, his small striped shirt covered in candy stains and his mouth in chocolate ice cream. They walked towards the playground until it became visible to the eye.
"There's the dragon" Jorge said as he pointed to the playground with large monkey bars that curved up and down with a head and antennas at the end, simulating a worm.
"Is that the dragon?" asked the tall man.
"Yes, that's the dragon" said Jorge.
"Ah, OK" said the officer nodding in surprise. "Of course that's the dragon" he said.

Rosita was walking a desperate walk. The police told her the bad news, only three out of one hundred kids are recovered if they're lost. She continued walking and saw a large man in the distance with a police hat. She focused and squinted and saw he was holding hands with a small boy. She ran as fast as she could until she recognized her boy.

"Jorge, Jorge" she started screaming.

She came close and the officer order her to stop.

"You stop right there" he said with a stern voice that the boy never heard from his friend before. "Jorge, do you recognize this woman?" he asked him crouching down to meet his size.

"Yes, that's my mother" said the boy.

"What is her name?" asked the man.

"Her name is Rosa Sandoval" he answered, without missing a beat.

"Ma'am, can I see some identification please?" he didn't let go of the boy.

She was stupefied, blinking and wiping her tears. She calmed herself down and pulled out every identification she had in her purse to erase any doubt. She even showed him photos of her and the boy she kept in her wallet.

Once the man was convinced of her identity, he let the boy go. She hugged him and held him in her arms.

"Why are you crying mother?" asked the boy.

The policeman chuckled.

I Saw the Sign

Rosita knew when it was time to go back home and this was the time. This was a sign, she was convinced, and she didn't need more than one sign to take a hint. It was time to fix the custody problem and go back to Tijuana. Rosita spent hours, days and weeks giving thanks to God and the

Guardian Angel that kept her boy safe. The boy didn't even know he was ever lost or in any danger.

For weeks, Rosita meditated on solutions for fixing her custody problem with the boy's father. She called friends, spoke with lawyers, yet nothing seemed to work. She decided to take it all the way to the top. She was in Mexico City anyway.
"I will go to Los Pinos and fix this once and for all" she told herself.

Los Pinos is the compound that hosts the presidential home and president's office. Rosita was a tough and bold young woman, yet she was also embarrassedly innocent of mind. But it was hard to talk her out of it. Flor, her elderly roommate tried to, and so did her friends and colleagues from work. "You're crazy, you can't go to the President's house, you'll get arrested. Add that to your list of problems" said her brother. But what did she have to lose? Desperate times right?!

Rosita put on her best summer dress that day and a small suit on her son. She fixed her hair and makeup as if she was attending a Royal Ball. She wrote a letter that she would give to the guard or the secretary or whomever stopped her from going in. "Maybe the letter would make it all the way to the president and he would fix my custody problem" she thought. "Maybe I'll even give it to him personally".

Rosita prepared for her meeting and dressed up her boy in his most formal clothes. She walked to the metro station and after a short ride, she emerged to take a bus to the presidential home. To her surprise the gate was open and the armed soldiers where letting people in. As she got closer, she noticed a long line of people waiting their turn to go in. The guards checked their invitation and searched for them in a list before allowing anyone to enter. She stood at the back of the long line of people waiting to get inspected, looking left and right at everyone shuffling in at a slow pace with the flow. She quickly noticed every couple had an invitation. Some were using it as a fan against the mid-day sun.

"Hi darling" a soft, kind-sounding voice came from behind. She turned to see a woman accompanied by her husband and what looked to be their daughter, about the same age as her. She was well-dressed with a pink dress and a fashionable hat.

"Hello, good afternoon" said Rosita turning and smiling showing her teeth. The boy extended his hand saluting all three of them with a hand shake.

"What is this? What a well behaved young man" said the lady leaning forward to shake the small hand. The boy smiled and looked up at his mother.

"My name is Luz, this is my daughter Maria Luisa and my husband Juan Carlos. Are you going to the party?" Maria asked smiling, holding her purse in both hands and looking very motherly.

"Yes, well no, not really, I don't have an invitation. I came to speak with the president" she said. Then realized how naïve that sounded.

The woman smiled as did her husband, now paying attention at the conversation.

"Why do you need the president?" said Luz.

Rosita proceeded to tell the tale of her ex-husband and how he bribed a judge to get custody of her son. How she ran away and exiled herself to Mexico City to hide from him and how he abused her, submitting her to what the couple thought was slavery by the time she told her story.

As she spoke Rosita fought tears. The memories were still fresh and retelling them was as if she was reliving them. She fought the tears. Her boy could not see them, besides, it would ruin her make-up.

The trio looked at each other in disbelief. Maybe it was the story, maybe it was looking at this young woman standing her thinking she could see the president. Or maybe it was the fact she told her account quickly and nonchalant. Very as a matter of fact, as a problem needing of a remedy.

The lady blinked and stared at Rosita, then the boy, then again to her husband. "You're coming with us" she said very determined.

As they approached the gate, they flashed their invitation. "Party of five" she said. The guards looked at the invitation and checked her ID comparing it to their list. They saw a discrepancy. It was probably the party of five part. Rosita gulped in desperation. She had her letter ready.

Holding it tightly on her left hand and her son on the other. Ready to give the letter to the guard in case she couldn't get through. "At least they could pass it up along the chain and maybe it will get to him" she thought. Luz stood still, her purse hanging from her left arm. Both guards looked at the people in the party. One older male, one female on the list, and probably her daughters and small grandson. "Welcome to Los Pinos" one of the guards said. Please follow the others in that direction. He pointed to where all other guest where walking.

"Yes, thank you" said Luz. "I know the way". She looked back at Rosita and winked a happy wink. "Come on love, let me introduce you to one of my friends, she's an old friend of mine and might be able to help".

Rosita never got to meet the president. She didn't even get to see him. Instead she met someone better, a mother, someone who immediately understood and cared for her situation, the first lady. Luz was an old friend of hers and one phone call from the first lady fixed the problem immediately and permanently. Rosita returned with her family and never left again. Well, only for vacation.

The World Turns

Twenty-five years later, Rosita received a phone call at home.

"I'm looking for Rosa Sandoval" a woman said on the other side of the phone.

"Who's looking for her?" asked Rosita, ever vigilant.

"I'm calling to see if she's the daughter of Mr. Horacio Sandoval" said the voice.

"Yes, this is Rosa Sandoval. How can I help you?" said Rosita.

"We found your father on the street homeless and he told us he had a daughter in Tijuana by your name, so we called you using the white pages" she said.

Rosita wasted no time. She took a plane the very next day to Puebla in the south of Mexico to go see her father. His legs were amputated and he could hardly see, the results of years of untreated diabetes.

He was in an old medical clinic outside Puebla in a small town run by nuns. The nuns picked him up out of the street and took him to the hospital where they amputated his legs "Rosita, my angel" said Horacio.

She took him by the hand and touched his face. "What are you doing here?" said Rosita to her father.

"This is my retirement villa" he said waiving to the room in a majestic gesture.

She laughed and shook her head. "Oh dad, you're still the same".

"Only shorter" he said laughing.

Rosita laughed and so did the nun.

"Come closer my baby so I can see you" said Horacio.

Rosita got closer and her father held her face with both hands, pulling her closer.

"Oh my baby, my beautiful baby, my Guardian Angel" he said breaking down in tears of regret, tears of sorrow, and tears of disbelief.

Rosita moved her father to a private home near the ocean, half an hour from her own home. She got private medical care for him but he lost his sight that same year. After a year, Horacio moved into Rosita's home where she and a nurse took care of his meals and all of his needs. Horacio lost all of his money, his friends, his second wife left him and his other children didn't want anything to do with him. Life was not kind to him in the past few years. He went from being a millionaire to homeless, alone, and forgotten. Now blind and with no legs, in a wheelchair, at the mercy of the daughter he had abandoned twice. First as a child breaking her heart and leaving her homeless, the second time also leaving her homeless but with a heart so big it could no longer be broken.

Two years passed and Horacio counted his blessings every morning.

"I'm sorry, forgive me" he said to her daughter Rosita every day when he saw her. He often cried for a few minutes holding her hand.

"There's nothing to forget" she always answered.

"You are my Guardian Angel, by beautiful baby" he told her in tears.

Horacio died later that year. Loved by his daughter, in her house, in his sleep.

My First Angel

Some childhood memories pop in and out of my head. Very specific ones are of my time living in La Escondida neighborhood. It was a quaint little place where my grandmother, my mother and I lived. Before that, my uncles and aunts lived there as well but those memories are not as prevalent. Most days I played by myself in the yard among the dirt, the grass and the ants. My action heroes, cars and imaginary friend were the rule of the land.

One Saturday, I rose early in the morning as kids do. Not wanting to wake up the house, I sneaked outside without making a sound, walking through the hallway with tennis shoes in one hand and a skateboard in the other, wearing shorts and a ripped t-shirt. I had to sneak out and walk all the way to the street because I needed the cement sidewalk to ride my skateboard. The street was thirty yards from my front door so I knew my mother would not hear me outside playing as I didn't want to wake her. I exited the small community through a wooden door attached to a cement wall five foot tall, painted in white. The wall wasn't very high, but when you're only four years old it's a very tall wall. I closed the wooden door behind me and it clicked when the metal mechanism found its partner.

Only a few minutes after trying my first skateboard trick, a car pulled over to the curve just in front of me. I turned to look at the only running car in an otherwise silent street. I was immediately suspicious. You might erroneously think that a small boy of four years, skinny as your pinky finger with long hair, reference of a hippy mother, doesn't even see the word suspicious. On the contrary. My mother took excellent care to turn me into a young Sherlock Holmes. Observing the landscape to spot any incoming trouble. She used to train me in kidnapping response since the age of three. Running drills where she approached me in a car and tried to offer me candy "little boy, come here and take some candy" she would say and I had to run away in the opposite direction the car was driving. This was only one of the drills, we had several that we practiced at least once per month. Paranoid you say? Only if they're not chasing you!

"Why do we practice so much?" I asked her one day. "I already know what to do".
"One day someone will try to offer you candy and pull you into the car, or they will follow you after school and you have to spot them" she said.
"Why would someone pull you into their car?" I used to think. But I knew the answer. They will steal you away from your family. I didn't know why, but I knew they would do it.

The problem is that at the age of four you're lacking an internal danger meter. You don't have that thing inside you that tells you people can be bad, or people are inherently bad, or not all people are good. When you're four years old, you don't have that knowledge. That's why you're innocent.

When the car pulled over, I glanced up to recognize the driver. Maybe it was a neighbor. No, it was a stranger. The man leaned over the passenger seat and rolled down the window of the passenger side. I froze in place letting the skateboard roll down the sidewalk.
"Hello, maybe you can help me" the strange man said.
My eyes widened and I looked down the street again. It was completely empty of movement and sound. "I have to be polite. I have to help people" I thought. "Maybe he's looking for someone and there's nobody on the street to help him. Or maybe he's looking for my neighbor and I can tell him where he lives." All thoughts crossed my mind in an instant. I stood in place, holding my hands letting the skateboard escape me, and ideas running in my head like a hamster.

The man repeated himself. "Maybe you can help me" he said. I looked at him without reacting. "I'm looking for someone who lives around here" he said while reaching for the door handle.

"Run" I heard an alarm emanating from my big toe going up my entire body until it reached the tip of my hair. "Run Jorge run" I heard the voice as clear as my thoughts today. The man jerked the door handle to get the door open on the driver side.

My eyes got wide and my tiny heart pushed against my chest once, twice, three times. I looked left and I looked right. The quiet street now meant a lack of help, nobody was there to witness the event, to help me, to get my mother. My eyes searched for the man. He was now pushing the door open with a rusted screech, his left foot touched the asphalt and he thrusted himself out of the car. I couldn't breathe, my feet felt swallowed by the cement sidewalk. I looked down at them to see why they weren't moving. They weren't in the cement. I looked back up to search for the man. It seemed he was moving in slow motion, running around the back of the car towards me. "Run!" A terrified panicking voice screamed in my head like an unwelcomed alarm clock. A burst of adrenalized energy hit me in half a second and traveled down my arms and legs like electricity. I woke from my paralyzed state with what felt like fifty cups of coffee running up and down my skin like fire ants.

The adrenaline overdose woke me up, showing me this was not a dream. "Breathe" I heard the voice in my head and I obeyed, taking a deep breath, a breath I'd been holding in all this time. The man was almost on top of me, a towering

59

figure reaching with terrible hands filed with greed and terror. I turned around and took three steps towards the wall standing a whole foot taller than me. I continued running placing my left foot on the wall and jumped to grab on to the top of the wall with the tip of my fingers. I then took three more steps while walking to reach the top. Once my chest cleared the top of the wall I pulled myself up with my wire hanger arms until the top of the wall was under my belly. I looked at the dirt floor on the other side. I had to dive for it head first with no time to turn around to land on my feet. I launched myself forward towards the floor trying to avoid rocks on either side of the dirt and pushed myself forward and then down, making a dive for safety. I almost made it all the way.

As I was freefalling I felt a giant hand grab my shoe and part of my right leg. I didn't hit the floor; I hit the wall with my entire body as both his hands now grabbed my foot. He started pulling me up and back towards him. I almost made it all the say. Now I was hanging upside down, arms flapping, trying to grab something to pull myself down. I started to scream hysterically. I don't remember what I screamed but it had to be terrifying and horrific because my neighbor's son, a young man on the heavy side with broad shoulders and wavy long hair came out with a bat in his hand. At that moment the man holding me let go with one hand to try and unlock the metal pin on the wooden door with his free hand. His grip weakened and my foot left my shoe. I hit the floor with my hands and then my head. He staggered back with my shoe in his hand.

My neighbor started screaming profanities at the man while running through his porch towards him, waving his bat aggressively. The awful man let go of the shoe and ran around his car to the driver's side door, jumped in with new found agility, turned the key and did a U-turn to leave the scene. But before my neighbor managed to use his car as a piñata, he broke one of his windows all while screaming at him from the top of his lungs. The neighbors started to come out of their houses to see what was happening. My neighbor ran down the street pursuing the car still screaming. I was crying uncontrollably waiting for my neighbor to come back from his pursuit. The other neighbors gathered around me and delivered me to the safety of my mother's arms. This was a very close call, my first one, but not my last one.

I've had two guardian angels in my life. Well, that I know of. The first I had as a child. Not sure from what age but I remember speaking with him, or her. I think it was a "her". I remember seeing my guardian angel in vivid dreams where I was floating out of my bed. But I mostly remember her when I was playing outside in the dirt. I was a four year old having hour long conversations about what's important to a four year old.

"Who are you talking too" my grandmother asked when she used to hear my conversations.

"My friend" I always answered.

"How cute" they probably thought, "he has an imaginary friend".

I don't remember my exact conversations. I do remember we built little dirt roads and played with my toy car for hours using my imagination and chatting away with my friend. I also remember my friend lecturing me quite often. Not like a grown up would lecture, or a teacher, it was very different, like another child lecturing me, a genius child that knows everything, but can still communicate to another child in the same language. My friend was not always there, talking and talking. It was mostly when I was alone, playing, thinking. As an only child living with a working mother and grandmother, I was very often alone.

The Weenie Taco Secret Recipe

The last day as a six-year-old was the first time I had to walk to school. Happy Birthday to me! It wasn't a short walk around the corner. It was a half an hour walk each way. Walking slowly watching all the plants and the doors, playing with dogs and cats, I would always find on the way. More than once I took them home and hid them under my bed. Sometimes I think my family was crazy allowing a small boy to walk that distance every day, but when you work two jobs you do what you have to do.

When I got home from school I was always hungry but there was no one at the house. I came up with what I thought was a smart solution. I would make weenie tacos. It was not as simple as I thought. Turning on the stove was the big problem. I was afraid of fire, or more accurately, I was afraid of burning my hand. The solution? I grabbed an entire page of the newspaper and rolled it up tight. Then used a lighter to light the tip of the rolled newspaper and slowly turned the gas knob clockwise and took two steps back while extending my arm holding the burning newspaper towards the gas. I can still remember the sound of the gas coming out of the stove with a faint whistle. Then the burning newspaper hitting the gas with a pop as it ignited and startled me every time. Now the dilemma of extinguishing the newspaper. It's not as easy as it sounds. Yes, sometimes I just took a deep breath and blew it out like an oversized birthday candle. But that didn't always work. One time, I opened the water faucet and dropped the paper on the sink. At least once per week, the flame burned too fast and I had to drop it to the kitchen floor and quickly stomp it out in a frantic march.

Now I had fire. The caveman probably had an easier job discovering fire than me as a boy producing it from our old heavy stove. After this great accomplishment, I took a weenie, stuck a fork into it and held it over the flame. The fork gave me the distance I needed not to get burned but I had to be careful not to heat up the fork and burn my fingers. One more step and I was done, heat up the tortilla.

Flower tortillas were the favorite at my house, handmade by my grandmother and brought into shape without a roller. The technique is simple, throw the tortilla into the open flame like a flying disk and turn it with a fork once, twice, and done. There you have it, the secret recipe for a seven-year-old to prepare a weenie taco.

Bus Money

Can you imagine a seven-year-old boy playing with fire? That's nothing, I used to take the bus at age nine. Not the school bus or the public bus that stops at the corner. This was the regular transit bus in Tijuana, and I still had to walk a mile after my stop. My mother taught me how to take the bus in a very ingenious way. First we both took the bus and I paid the driver to gain some confidence. Then we took the next bus back. Busses transit every two or three minutes through the main boulevard so you can jump on one with almost no wait. After my confidence was up, my mother walked me to the bus stop but I walked up the stairs and paid the driver by myself. My mother told him to drop me off at the next stop and took the next bus to meet me there. I was instructed to exit the bus and wait for my mother. This is how you teach a small child to take the bus on their own in a busy, dangerous city.

I remember one particular time I took the bus home when I was nine years old. When on the bus, I usually searched for a window seat and stared out the window the entire bus ride, counting the blocks and looking for familiar buildings and landmarks so that I knew where I was at all times and how long I had until my bus stop. That was my bus ride technique so not to miss my stop. This particular time I was so sleepy I was nodding my head unconsciously as I drifted into sleep for half a second after waking up abruptly when my head fell limp. The fifth or sixth time I woke up and did not recognized the street, the buildings or anything framed by the window. I looked to a stranger sitting next to me. She was a middle aged woman with grocery bags at her feet.

"Did we pass the 5 and 10?" I asked. A popular landmark that happened to be my stop.

"Oh yes, about half an hour ago" she said.

I stood up immediately and pulled the string that rang the bell signaling a stop. "Ding" it sounded once. I pulled again, "Ding" it sounded a second time. I leaped over the woman with the groceries as she moved her knees out of the way and headed for the door. I was holding my tears in so nobody would see.

The bus stopped and I jumped out crying as soon as I hit the sidewalk. I looked both ways without recognizing anything. "What should I do?" I thought hiding my tears from strangers passing on the sidewalk. I had my emergency one peso to call from a public phone and I would use it to dial my mom at her work. There was a line of three people to use the public phone. I stood in line between adults and waited my turn, my school backpack hanging from one shoulder. Three more people stood behind me in line. By the time it was my turn I had five people behind me. I felt the pressure to make my call quickly.

I knew the number by memory and I dialed it fast. I explained to Mom what happened, crying even more as soon as she answered the phone. She listened patiently and tried to calm me down. After a few seconds I did, and now it was time for a solution.

"Cross the street and take another bus home" she said.

"Dah Mom" I thought. That's not a solution.

"What do I do?" I asked again.

"You're OK, just cross the street and take a bus the other way" she repeated.

The solution was so easy. Just cross the street and take the bus the opposite direction to your stop. Sounded easy enough. But when you're young and crying you just want your mother, not another bus ride.

"I don't have any money" I told her.

"You can ask someone on the street for some. It's an emergency they'll understand" my mother said.

"Ask for money" I thought. "How will I do that?" I tried to think for alternatives. "Maybe she can pick me up" I thought. That idea vanished as I remember she was at work and we didn't own a car anymore. I started crying again, silently, looking down and hiding under the phone booth embarrassed for making people wait in line, and for crying in public.

"Calm down" my mom said. "It's ok it's not your fault. Just take another bus back and it will be fine".

I didn't want to hang up the phone but I knew the others behind me wanted to use the phone. I had to finish up and get back to reality.

"Ask for money, take the bus and call me when you get home" she said.

At that time, I could hear the sound, "bip, bip, bip" that meant your time was up. Either you deposit another coin into the phone or you'll be cut off.

"OK Mother, bye". And with a click I returned the phone to its resting place.

I wiped my tears on my sleeve and wanted to get away as quickly as I could from the phone. The people in line probably saw me weeping. I reluctantly turned my head back to see if they were looking at me and felt intense dark eyes fixed on me, a young woman was staring without a blink. I'm not sure how young anymore; when you're a child everyone past the age of twelve looks old. She reached out with her pale fingers and gave me a coin. It was enough for the bus. A large five peso coin if I remember correctly. Soles or Sun's we used to call those coins. The young lady looked vaguely familiar. She didn't say anything; she smiled without showing her teeth, she smiled more with her eyes than with her mouth. "Gracias" I said with a knot in my throat and embarrassed both for crying and for accepting money from a stranger. I clinched the coin with my small hand tightly, as if losing it would be a catastrophe. For me it probably would. I looked at my hand holding the coin and then back up, her smiling eyes still looking down at me with amusement, without saying a single word. She winked, and I left.

Still sobbing, I ran to the corner with my back pack on my back and my new coin in hand and crossed the street to catch the bus on the other side. It was the city's main road back then, a busy boulevard that crossed from one point of the city to another. I was very careful crossing the busy street and looked at everyone suspiciously. I managed to stop crying before the next bus made the stop two minutes later. Buses were always filled to the max with standing room only. Many times you had to pay at the front of the bus, exit, and then run to the back to get in through the back door. Sardines have more space to move than some of those busses.

Thirty years later I was at my home entertaining some friends. We were outside barbecuing chicken and vegetables. Now living in the USA, my friends were telling me how their kids don't even know how to cross the street. "It's embarrassing, and dangerous" they said. Remembering our adventures as kids in Tijuana. "Crossing the street is nothing" I told them. "Let me tell you how I used to take the bus as a kid" and I proceeded telling them the story.

I love telling stories, so I was trying to make it as entertaining as possible. Making them laugh telling them when I was falling asleep at the bus and how my Mother told me to ask for money. As I came to the part of the young woman handing me a coin I felt chills creeping up from my spine all the way through my arms into my fingertips as her image popped into my head. I've never before told this story and never tried to recall the details of the encounter. "I know this person" I thought. I know this girl from somewhere. I remembered her not as a long lost friend, not as someone you encounter after some years of not seeing them. It was more like when you see the son or brother of your friend and you know they're related. You don't actually know them, but the way they talk, walk, their stare, it all reminds you of someone. That's the way I felt at that moment. I took a deep breath and remembered my old childhood imaginary friend. "Gracias" I said to nobody, with a grin.

I wish I knew who my childhood Guardian Angel was. It would be a great conversation. I would ask about how she got there, how she managed to play with me for hours day after day after day for years. What her goals were, if she's happy or what brings her happiness. Did she choose me or was I an assignment? She was so friendly, so patient and a great listener. I thought she was a child when I was one myself. Or maybe she was a child and grew up with me. I'm not sure, the young woman who gave me the coin was older than me. Well, I don't know the rules. I just know my first angel was more like a body guard, a protector, a real guardian. Much like the ones you see portrayed in paintings or stories. A larger than life angel with big wings behind a child, spreading his wings to protect the child from the world. That's how I felt growing up. As if I had a tall angel hovering around me making sure I didn't get kidnapped, stabbed or worse. And it happened more than it should, I think I got more than my fair share of scares from the first time until I was twenty one years old. You see, all that time I walked to school, had to take public transportation in bad neighborhoods, later on I had to cross the border to San Diego and take public transportation to the university and back, passing through the not so desirable streets of Tijuana at night. When you're walking the worse streets of Tijuana every single day for fifteen years, something is bound to happen.

My first Guardian Angel didn't have wings, she didn't glow or appear dressed in robes. I didn't even know what she was at the time, other than my imaginary friend. The other Guardian Angel I remember is my current one. I'm not sure what happened to my childhood angel. Maybe she's here with me, or with another assignment. I'm not sure. I don't see her, hear her or feel her. Could she be with me still? Maybe I have two angels, or maybe she only guards children. My current angel was more of a request from my board of advisers. Wait, I think you need to know what that is and how they are important, and how you should also build your own board of advisors. We'll talk more about that in other stories.

PART II: LOST AND FOUND

How lucky we are to find what we never knew we lost…

The 4 O'clock Dolphin Show

"Be ready by twelve" I told my cousin Christian over the phone. "Make sure you bring some shorts and t-shirts". Christian is only one year younger than me, as tall as me, thin as your toothbrush if your toothbrush had light brown curly hair.

"All right" Said Christian in an excited voice. "But, I don't have shorts or t-shirts" His voice had a tone of confusion as he was not sure if I was joking. I always made fun of his semi-formal big city dress.

"Dude!" I said "You need your summer threads, I'm talking about your board shorts, flip flops, your tank top, the whole ensemble".

"Really?" He asked as if waiting for a set-up.

"Dude" I said again in a joking tone to through him off even more. "We'll be in front of the beach for three whole days. It will be just us, the sand and the water. No houses, no obstacles. Pure unadulterated beachfront property".

Now he was sure I was joking!

"So you want to pick me up dressed as a surfer?" He asked in good humor with his usual deep and merry voice.

"You got it baby" I said. "And don't be late or we're going to miss the dolphin show" He bursted in laughter.

"The dolphin show?" He asked to see what else I would come up with.

"Yes man" I said. "The dolphin show - It's at 4 PM every day so we can't be late cause you forgot to buy shorts".

His laugh was loud and contagious over the speaker. I looked at my wife that was next to me and winked. She smiled and shook her head.

I was smiling knowing he was not buying my story. He probably thought he was being set up for a practical joke. "Now let me speak to your pops" He put my uncle on the line.

"It's Jorge" Christian said while handing over the phone to his father.

"Hello helloo" My uncle answered the phone.

"What's up uncle Pepe?" I asked.

"Hanging here with Christian" He said. Uncle Pepe is a smooth, cool operator.

"Hey Uncle -make sure Christian buys some shorts, flip flops and t-shirts before I pick him up. I don't want him on the beach with his thick wool pans, long sleeve shirt and hush puppies".

"Ja-ja-ja" He laughed. "You got it Jorgillo - what time will you pick him up?"

"We'll be there tomorrow at twelve" I said.

"Got it. I'll go shopping with him. See you then, bye" -He hung up.

I put down my cell phone and turned to Gloria smiling "Dude doesn't believe me we're in front of the beach" She laughed happily. "He doesn't believe there's a dolphin show" I told her shrugging and smiling. "He doesn't even believe he needs to buy shorts". She was now laughing out loud. "Can you imagine him in shorts?" I asked her. "He probably never used shorts in his life!"
"Come on" She said. "He has beaches a few hours from Mexico City and I know he's been in Acapulco many times".
"Not in shorts". I said.

Gloria and I packed for the weekend getaway. We were going to my Aunt Sonia's and Uncle Miguel's place down in San Antonio only 30 minutes or so from the San Diego, Tijuana border. This is a favorite hangout for us and we always stayed a couple of days with my uncles; even if my cousins weren't there. Even though my uncles have 20 and 30 years on us we've become better and better friends over the years.

The next morning was one of those many gorgeous days with the sun coming up at eighty degrees Fahrenheit. "Thank God" I said as I usually say when opening my bedroom window. "I love San Diego". We threw our small bags in the trunk of the car and headed out stopping at the supermarket for food and lots of beer.

Our house is only twenty minutes from the USA/Mexico border so we crossed quickly and drove to pick up Christian. He saw us coming up the hill. I could see his wild curly hear standing straight up as if by magic peeking out the window.

We didn't even finish parking when Christian busted out of the house wearing the most ridiculous outfit. "What-the!" I looked at Gloria with eyes wide and already laughing uncontrollably. She was getting out of the car smiling and reached out for a hug as he was running to greet us.
"Hello guys I'm ready. How do you like my rags?" he asked us in a serious tone, smiling while bobbling his head. We hugged him laughing and Gloria asked "Where did you go shopping?"
"I had no time so I went to the pharmacy down the street at the 5 and 10" he said.
"5 and 10?" Gloria looked at him with an incredulous look.
"Yes, 5 and 10". He said. "Isn't that what you call it?"
"Yea, I guess so". She shrugged. "But I didn't even know they sold clothes there".

I was still laughing when my uncle Pepe came out to say goodbye. 5 and 10 is an old pharmacy deep in the heart of Tijuana near my old house, where Uncle Pepe lived at the moment. It wasn't a shopping mall or story or anything like that.

Christian was wearing a black bowling shirt with colorful red and yellow flames at the bottom with a wife beater underneath and Bermuda flaming shorts going down to his white bonnie knees. That combined with his new found flip-flops and his curly long hail sticking up in the air as usual, made for a comical but very welcome sight.

"Am I ready or not?" he said. "I'm practically a California surfer boy ha?" He extended his long wiry arms up in the air for effect and then looked down at his outfit with pride and a little disbelief. "I would have never imagined myself in these clothes". He said.

"Welcome to the family" I said. "Now get in the car we don't want to be late for the 4 o'clock dolphin show".

Christian brought his hands in front of his face and shrugged while asking "Is he still going on with his dolphin show? Is there even a beach where we're going?" he asked.

"Yes, there's a beach". Gloria told him.

"Now get in the car". I said. "We don't want to be late for the dolphin show".

Christian smiled and grabbed his weekend back-pack. We said goodbye to my uncle and we all got in the car headed to San Antonio del Mar.

We talked and joked on the way. We were all smiling the whole way there. Telling stories and planning the weekend, what we would eat, drink, read or play. Once in a while, Christian asked again "So is there really a beach were we're going?"

Gloria just laughed but did not answer. "You'll see" she said.

As we entered the gated community we drove through the unusually thin pebbled roads making it shortly to the house. "We're here". Gloria announced.
We all got out of the car and grabbed our bag plus some groceries and walked the short twenty feet to the front door. I was opening the front door with the key and I look back to say something and... Christian was not there. His stuff was left on the floor and he was gone.
Gloria made it to the door and asked "Where's Christian?"
"Don't know" I answered.
We quickly walked another twenty feet to the edge of the property with a backdrop to a sandy beach and saw Christian running full speed through the sand taking off his bowling shirt and kicking of his flip flops while diving head first into the pacific ocean's waves. He jumped and dove again and again like a little kid. Gloria and I stared at him and then at each other giggling like children. I shrugged my shoulders and headed back to put our bags and groceries away.

A few minutes later Christian came out of the water and walked up the stairs to the house.
"So Christian" I was waiting for him with a big grin on my face.
"Did I lie or what?" I asked him.

"Oh man this is incredible; right in front of the beach". He said. His hair was all wet and his curly hair was not slinking up anymore. Gloria was laughing as she put the groceries in the refrigerator.

"I told you it was right in front of the ocean" I said still grinning taking a mental photograph of him and the moment.

"Yes but I don't know when to believe you anymore" he said.

"You'll get to know him more" said Gloria.

My long lost cousin

My family is very close and I've always considered myself "born lucky". I was born lucky because of being brought into this loving big extended family. This whole cousin Christian story started only one year before the beach weekend getaway when I received a strange phone call from a woman. I was still living in Tijuana, Mexico at the time.

"Is Antonio there?" said the woman.

Antonio? I thought. Nobody calls Uncle Pepe Antonio. His name is Jose Antonio Sandoval and Pepe is a popular Mexican nickname for carriers of the name Jose.

"No" I said. "May I ask who is calling?"

"Yes, this is Pilar, I'm looking for Rosa's and Sonia's brother named Antonio" she clarified.

"Yes, that's the one" I said.

"Do you know when he'll be back?" she asked.

I was now suspicious. My uncle lived in the USA not in Tijuana, especially not at my house.

"No I don't know" I said. "May I take a message?"

"Does he live there?" She asked.

"Maybe I can help you with something" I said diverting the question. I'm a little paranoid by nature and all my years of living in Tijuana did not help. Now when I say a little paranoid I really mean a lot!

"I'm an old friend" She said. "I'll call Sonia and explain to her".

"Alright" I did not offer any other information or ask how she know my aunt Sonia, Uncle Pepe's sister.

"Bye".

"Good Bye" I said.

That was the end of it. I was a bit suspicious and called my aunt but did not find her. I would tell my uncle next chance to find out what all this was about.

The very next weekend I received another unexpected call from my Uncle Pepe. It was a sunny lazy Saturday morning and I was off from work spending the morning reading at home.

"Jorge good morning how are you?" said Uncle Pepe

"I'm well uncle how about yourself?"

"Also well. Is your mom around?" He asked.

"Yes, she's downstairs should I get her for you?"

"No, could you both pick me up at Pueblo Amigo near the border so we can go eat something? There's someone I would like you to meet". He said.

He probably crossed the border on foot and left his car on the US side.
"Sure thing let me just put something on and I'll be right there to pick you up". I quickly ran down the stairs to my mother's house and told her to get ready. We both got in the car and I drove to pick up my uncle.

As I approached the pick-up location I saw my uncle standing with two others. A young man, around 26 years old, only one or two years younger than me at that time, and a woman. Both my mom and I got out of the car and my mother recognized her immediately.
"Pili -how are you?" Said my mother as she hugged her tightly.
"This is my son Jorge".
"This is Christian" My uncle said with a faint grin and a big sparkle in his eyes. "He's my son". My mother and I looked at each other in deaf disbelieve. We've never seen this full gown man in our lives.
"I just found out". My uncle added shrugging and with his hands on his coat pockets.
"Well cousin" I said. "Welcome to the family". It felt right from the very first glance. As if I've known this kid all my life. He had a certain recognizable energy about him, an

energy I was used too. His entire demeanor felt familiar. It was familiar!

Later in conversation Pilar, Christian's mother, told me how Christian had been distant for the last couple of years.
"He's been depressed for some time" she confided. "He felt he did not fit in; as if he was different from me and the rest of his family. Even from his extended family. He was very uneasy and I was very worried" she told me.
"Is this why you decided to come here from Mexico City? I asked.
"Yes, that day I called I was going over the white pages looking for his father" she said. "I decided to tell Christian about his father and his other family. Your father is in Tijuana and you're just like him and his family, I told him a few days ago, and here we are. He wanted to come right away. I think his mood changed just from that new-found information. Look at him. He's happy" she said with the love only a mother can know about.
"Yes, and now I have a long-lost cousin that's been found" I told her.
"You're very alike you know" she said.
"I know" I answered.

And so, it came to be that I had a long lost cousin I didn't even know was lost until I found him!

Give Him a Show

Back at the beach house, Gloria was prepping flower tortilla quesadillas and Christian was helping her clean the kitchen. I stepped outside to bathe in the sun and breathe the warm Pacific Ocean air that was coming in like a blanket. What a beautiful moment, I thought.

From my spot on the large extended balcony I could see the entire solitary view of undisturbed sand and rhythmic waves producing white frothy foam. The sounds topped the experience with the crashing sounds that you only find with the perfect tide. "Oh, it's time" I thought. So I pulled up three outdoor plastic chairs next to each other facing the ocean. You couldn't see or hear a single human as for as far as the eye could manage. No neighbors in sight, as they only use their vacation homes one or twice per year.

"Hey guys; it's time". I called on them to come out. It was 4 o'clock sharp. The day still sunny and very hot.
"Time for what?". Christian asked thorough the kitchen window.
Gloria wiped her hands with a kitchen towel and came out while picking up her sunglasses on the way to her sitting spot.
"Time for the 4 o'clock dolphin show". I screamed back at him in exaggeration.
"Ja-ja-ja". He laughed. "You never give up".

Gloria sat next to me and took a deep breath.

"Come and see the show" I told Christian.

He stepped outside and strolled toward us. A large family of dolphins was passing through. Too many to count. Bobbing up and down as they came up for air. Dozens of them right in front of us and only a few feet from the sandy beach. Some of them playfully surfed the waves further entertaining us and making the experience even more remarkable. I looked at Christian. He was standing in disbelief with his mouth wide open and his hands up shading his eyes from the sun. He looked at me and Gloria and looked back at the site.

"Look at the babies swimming next to their mothers" he said.

I was glad I found my unknown long lost cousin. It was a special gift wrapped in a surprise. Getting another fully grown family member your age to love and share experiences with, emotions and life is something rare, something precious. So precious you can't buy it with any type of wealth and you can't win it in any type of contest. The lesson is in expectations. Life can surprise you and deliver much more than you can expect from it. It can give you priceless things. I closed my eyes and thanked god for his gift.

"Christian". He turned to face me. "Welcome to the 4 o'clock dolphin show".

What are Angels?

Holding a copy of my book transcript in her left hand, she looked at me suspiciously.

"Tell me what you know about Angels" She asked in what seemed to be friendly conversation over coffee.

Her husband, a dear and old friend of mine, glanced at me with a sneaky smile I recognized instantly. I nodded to him almost imperceptibly in both appreciation and acknowledgement. Smiling I tried to buy time. Doing my usual mental tally of what I knew about this person. Her intellect, education, prejudices.

"She can't be all that bad if she married my friend" I thought.

Now let me see: What are her religious inclinations, how religious is she anyway? Did she gather her religious knowledge at a religious education institution or at church?

After I tried to analyze all I could about what I know, I then assessed the consequences and damage control. Will she be angry? Would this escalate into an argument? Would the conversation cause problems for my friend after the party? Mind you, this is done in seconds or even less than seconds. The entire evaluation has to be done before I finish my grin. If I hold that grin too long, it starts looking creepy.

"Angels don't exist" I answer. "Please pass the cream".

"But you say you have a Guardian Angel" she protested trying to coax me into what I gathered was an argument.

"Yes I do", I answered simply.

"So then why do you say they don't exist?" She protested pointing at me with my own transcript with what I can only describe as a judgmental gesture.

"I say I have a Guardian Angel. I never said they exist" I answered once more. She was disappointed and shook her head but my friend gave her a stop gesture, so she didn't press the issue, at least not that day.

Having a philosophical, theological or even a lame religious discussion is not what I was looking for that day. Probably never with her, as I gather her religious prejudice and lack of education would prevent her from engaging in such a discussion. It sounds a bit harsh, but after a few of these conversations I tend to stay away unless I feel I can make a difference or learn something. Most other interactions I consider baiting from one side or the other looking for confirmation of their beliefs. If you need confirmation, than you need faith, whether you believe or you don't.

The History of Angels

I was visiting the San Diego Natural History Museum in Balboa Park on a beautiful Saturday afternoon. We have such beautiful afternoons almost every day in town, with perfect weather and pleasant people. My wife and I were very excited to see the traveling exposition of the Tomb of Tutankhamun. An exquisitely planned exhibit where you go from room to room witnessing the tomb chambers decorated exactly as explorer Howard Carter found them in 1923 in Thebes, Egypt.

After entering the recreation of the tomb chamber, I stood at the end of the sarcophagus for a few minutes. I stared with interest, I was perplexed. I saw an angel.
"What is an angel doing here?" I thought.
Yes, the tomb, 1,323 before Christ had depiction of what it looked to me a Guardian Angel. An angel that would guard the pharaoh in the afterlife for eternity I imagined or deduced. After all, why would it have an angel on the sarcophagus? Upon further exploration, I noticed the same angelical image was embossed into every corner of the outer case of the sarcophagus, a box like container holding the sarcophagus inside. This box had the angel in the four corners with the wings wide spread as in all the other images. The figures and wings covered the box almost entirely. This was a puzzling thought. Did the Egyptians believe in Angels?

If you're an Egyptian scholar you already know this. The images, I later found out, are of Isis. Isis is a Goddess of Life, Death and Rebirth. One of the most well-known Egyptian goddesses and adopted in many religions. The motherly symbolism attributed to life is well known all over the world from the ancient Mayan culture to the modern Catholics. Isis has been worshiped on earth for a very long time, longer than modern Christianity. From Egypt to Greece and the Roman Empire from around 3000 BC to 200 AD. In ancient mythology Isis represented the constellation of Virgo, or the Virgen, the Divine Mother whose child would be the savior of life, reminiscent of many other religions. There is no mistaking that religions interlay in their mythology, as there is no mistaking the images of Isis are those we now represent of Angels. With their wide spanned wings in a position of guardian over a powerful pharaoh.

Isis, also known as "Queen of the Heavens" is believed to be the first Egyptian goddess and mother of Horus, arguably the most important divinity in Egyptian history.

Sumerian Angels date back five thousand years before the Egyptians ever even thought of such beings to 8,000 BC. The Sumerian tablets from the library in Nippur account in their creation myth how the Annunaki fell from the sky. The Annunaki, or sons of Annu, god of the heavens, are the founders of the Sumerian culture. Enlightened beings that rocked the cradle of civilization that later was to be Mesopotamia.

Upon further research when leaving the museum, I discovered the Greeks took the angelical image of Isis from Egypt and created their own angelical images that appear in ancient pottery and artwork. They also had angel like winged gods including Nike, god of victory, and Eros, the winged child known as the god of love and his Roman counterpart Cupid. The same angelical images infiltrated Roman culture and mythology. After Emperor Constantine declared Christianity the official religion of Rome in 380 AD, the pagan images were simply adopted and incorporated in new religious art. The catholic religion persisted after the demise of the Roman Empire, and new medieval paintings incorporating angels spread throughout Western Europe. These evolved to become the standard images that we now associate with angels.

I Met My Spiritual Guide During a Backyard Party

Fray Hugo does not seem like a Giant at first glance. For one he's very short. He's also exaggeratedly hunched so he looks even smaller and shorter. He appears old and fragile, at least by the time I met him in Tijuana, Mexico. No, I did not meet Fray Hugo, a Franciscan monk, in a Nobel Peace Prize award, or in any kind of award ceremony. I did not meet Fray Hugo at an anthropology lecture about the Huichol indigenous population where he spent 50 years in the highest, coldest and most inhospitable mountains of Mexico. I did not even meet him in at the seminary or monastery. I met him of all places, in a backyard party, a BBQ in Tijuana. He doesn't look it, but this man is a Giant, and you would count yourself lucky if you could stand on his shoulders.

Sometimes you don't have to travel across the world to meet extraordinary people. Sometimes they're in your country, many times even in your state and I bet you have more than a handful in your city, even your neighborhood. If you're open, maybe they're in your family or will make it into your back yard. In this case I met Fray Kutchi at my sister in law's house in Tijuana. It was during a family reunion. It just so happens that Fray Kutchi is my father in law's brother. I didn't meet him before because he rarely leaves the high mountains of the Sierra Madre Occidental where his precious Huicholes live. Huicholes are a Native-American people of Mexico renegaded to some of the highest and most unhospitable spots in Mexico.

You'll notice my new uncle has several names. He's Fray Hugo, Fray Kutchi and his given name .... Gomez. Fray Hugo is the name he took after joining the Franciscan Monastery, leaving his old life and old name behind. Fray Kutchi is the name given to him by the Huicholes. It means "the old one".

As I entered the family reunion I saw Fray standing there with an old dusty baseball cap with the logo unrecognizable, a pair of very old sandals, maybe twenty years old, held together by tape and string, and a pair of jeans with a thick plaid cowboy shirt thinning down with age. I watched this unusual wizard like character out of the corner of my eye. Very curious to see this unique personality interact with the family he rarely sees, his old family, the ones not belonging to the monastery.

I was playing ball with one of the kids when Fray Kutchi approached me.
"Hello I'm Fray Hugo" he told me and extended his hand.

"I'm Jorge, Gloria's husband" I introduced myself and extended my hand in a hand shake.

He looked me sideways as if to look at me with his good eye. He had kind eyes the color of honey that felt just as sweet as they looked. He extended his hand and I shook it. It felt of old leather, skin wrinkled and aging, I could feel a hard life between my fingers. His long white beard fell down to his stomach like the sorcerous in the stories. At first glance Fray looked worn, tired, and retired. But when you looked deeper you realized it was all just a shell. His stare told you a different story, a story of love and service, of unintended sacrifice and overwhelming happiness. I wanted a part of those eyes.

We both sat down close to the grownups on a pair of children's pink chairs that the girls used to play their tea party. We sat at a distance from the rest of the party and talked for two hours without giving a thought to time or mortals. I then realized I was stealing him from the rest of his family and encouraged him to go back to the party. He wrinkled his nose and closed his eyes while moving his head in a "no" gesture. That's his patented move! We had a lot in common, and I found his life fascinating, bombarding him with one question after the next with little rest for water or breathing.

The life of a Franciscan Monk is not glamorous, especially one living in outmost isolation from civilization. He used to get invitations from universities and other anthropological organizations to lecture on the Huichol culture, but he always refused. "I belong in the Sierra" he said, referring to the mountain range where he resided for the last fifty years. "Why have you stayed so long in the mountains?" I asked Fray when I met him.

"Simple", he said, "I was milking a cow back in the monastery when I was a young man. My boss, the head of the Franciscans, came to me and said: Fray Hugo, I stood up and said: Yes Sir, while saluting like a soldier. Then he told me: I want you to go up to the mountains where the states of Jalisco, Durango, Zacatecas and Nayarit meet, called the four points. Yes Sir, I said again. When should I come back from there? I asked. You should stay there until I tell you to come back, he told me." Fray smiled and his eyes sparkled when he told me the story.

"When did he tell you go leave the mountains and back to the monastery?" I asked.

"He hasn't, that's why I'm still there after fifty years" he said.

"When do you think he'll ask you back?" I asked.

"Well, he died twenty years ago" he chuckled showing his missing front teeth. He set me up for the joke. Funny guy that monk!

This is the beginning of what made Fray Kutchi a Giant, and now a legend and inspiration in the Franciscan congregation.

"Come back with me to the mountains" he said. "Let me show you what I see every day."
After only ten minutes of meeting him I told him "Yes, I'll go with you to the mountains". I didn't know what I was getting in to.

"Let's take some pictures" someone said. Fray Hugo stood up and opened his tiny backpack. "Wait one minute" he said while he put on his Franciscan robe. A traditional thick brown robe tied at the waist with a rope and an oversized rosary hanging from the rope.

The Trip

It was a long trip to the mountains. You can now drive up to the region by car, before this you had to take a small plane and land in a very small strip the locals made by cleaning up a flat piece of land on top of one of the mountains. It took us eighteen hours by car after flying to Guadalajara in the state of Jalisco.
"Roads changed the landscape" Fray Kutchi told us. "There is influence from the whites and it's not all good" he said. Alejandra, my wife's sister and her husband Leo made the trip with us.

We prayed the entire way there. If Fray was awake, we were praying. It seemed every time we got in the car we prayed. We probably wore out his rosary! Before we got to the mission he told us the ground rules.

"You will wear a Franciscan cross on the outside of your clothing at all times" he said seriously. "You will not go out without me and you will not leave my side for more than ten paces". He said nodding with his index finger.

"Is it dangerous?" I asked.

"Not if you do what I say" he said. I didn't think this was much of an answer. Fray Kutchi gave many of these types of answers.

"How dangerous is it?" I asked again.

He smiled at my wife Gloria while pointing at me. "This one is always insisting" he said. They will not think twice about killing you. They don't trust you if you're not Huichol" he said.

"Oh great" I thought. "That's all I need". My wife gave me a glance, one of those scared ones.

"What is your name?"
"When did you get here?"
"When are you leaving?"

These were the three questions every child asked us during our stay in Huichol country up in the mountains of Mexico.

We arrived at the mission after dark. We couldn't see anything except for when we had our headlights on. It was pitch black all the time because there is no electricity until you come down the mountain many miles away in the next town. This wasn't a town; it wasn't a village or anything remote to it. It was just a small dwelling in the middle of nowhere. This is what Fray called "The Mission". It didn't look anything like a mission, or at least not what I had in mind. This was a very poor version of anything, especially a mission.

Leo was driving "I'll go closer to illuminate you with the headlights" he said. We all got out of the car and headed towards the mission, or the shack I should say. We walked atop the overgrown grass all around us. As we arrived to the shack Fray unlocked a padlock on a rusty metal door. "This is my room" he said "It's also the kitchen. I moved into the kitchen because it's too cold everywhere else". We walked into a small room barely ten feet across. I glanced around. There was almost nothing in there. I looked to the cabinet. It had two cans of tuna, a small jar of peanut butter half empty and for cooking a small camping stove with a tiny gas tank. The type you use for a one day adventure in your back yard.

The paint came down the walls long ago and it was falling down. It was very damp, with almost no food, freezing cold and very depressing. I looked over at my wife. Her large eyes jumped from behind her jacket's hood. She looked around and I heard a big "gulp" coming from her direction. She met my eyes and didn't blink. I could tell she was distressed. I winked at her. Alejandra and Leo made it in behind us "Wow" said Leo when he entered not masking his emotions. "Leo!" Alejandra got his attention and signaled at him to be quiet.

Fray walked a few paces to another door. "Here is my room" He said. We followed and picked into an adjacent room, or at least we thought it was a room. It was the bathroom.
"It's the warmest spot in the house so I moved in here ten years ago" he said.
It had a makeshift bed made up of blankets with more blankets on top. One extra shirt hung from a nail on the wall and a cowboy hat from another. All next to the toilet. My wife started crying and turned her head so Fray wouldn't see her. I got a heavy feeling in my bottom of my stomach.
"How can someone live like this?" I thought.

Fray lived off the land. He received no charity, he asked for none either. There was no supermarket or store, so he cultivated corn, potatoes, pumpkins and other vegetables. He had little protein except for milk during the short periods he owned a cow. His drinking water was dirty. I told everyone to boil the water before drinking it. I was sure it was filled with parasites.

The following few days we spent all our time learning about him and the Huicholes. How they live, their belief system, how they interacted with Fray. We also asked about Fray, and he never ran out of stories to tell us. When they almost killed him, when they almost ate him, when he got bit by a scorpion, a snake, and lots of other stories.

We all drove over the mountains to every home and every tribe and community around five surrounding mountains. Everyone knew Fray. Men, woman and children smiled when they saw him pass by. Fray built schools and demanded teachers from the government. He cured children and delivered newborns. He taught old and young to read and to cultivate the land. He also defended the rights and property of all the indigenous population. And he did it all alone, one man in the mountains, dressed in funny robes with a funny wizard beard. All while praying.

"I'm so happy to be a Fray" he told me every day as if he forgot telling me the day before. He wrinkled his nose and squinted his eyes while nodding slowly. "I'm so happy to be here". Can you imagine? How can he be happy? Living in conditions that made my wife cry, not having enough food or water and being alone for fifty years. How come he looks like the happiest man I've ever seen? How come he never left the mountains unless commanded by his superior? His superior that died thirty years back.

"You think I'm alone but I'm not" he told me in a whisper. The way he liked speaking to me, as if he was telling me the secrets of the universe and nobody else could listen. "You think I'm poor but I'm not". He said smiling showing his missing teeth. I knew what he was going to say before he said it, and I felt ignorant and spiritually empty for not comprehending. "God is with me here in the mountains and I'm so happy to be of service to him" he said in his whispering way.

I learned many things from Fray Kutchi. Most importantly what a happy person looks like. We need to redefine the term happiness. It's not what we have in our pocket but in our soul. He had a light in his soul that could not be extinguished. Happiness is closing your eyes for ten seconds and nodding "Yes, I have everything".

During the trip, we visited villages, other missions, a Franciscan school for small and very adorable Huichol children, and got to spent time with Fray. We had an emotional connection, something inspired me from his life, from his eyes, from his spirit. I left Fray a better man and returned to the city.

One year later, we got on a plane to attend Fray's fiftieth anniversary of being a Franciscan Monk. It was a beautiful mass in Fray Kutchi's favorite church in the closest town to the ranch where he grew up. A town called Santuario. He had a beautiful mass given by eight priests and attended by the highest Franciscan monks in the country.
"Fray Kutchi is a living legend" they all said.
The surprise was a busload of Huichol Indians that made it all the way from the mountains. They looked beautiful in their traditional clothes. Men wearing cotton hand knitted

and embroidered by their mothers or wives. Women and girls have traditional pink skirts and blue, yellow and white blouses that make the colors even brighter against their dark skin. More than twenty Huicholes made the trip to celebrate Fray's anniversary. He was so happy to see them.

"You have to come back and stay for a year" Fray told me after his mass.
"Yes Fray, I will. I'll come back and stay a year with you" I told him.
He died soon after. I never got to go back.

Time passed and I found myself again on an airplane with my sisters in law, my wife and my father in law headed to Guadalajara towards the beautiful Franciscan Basilica of Our Lady of Zapopan (Basilica de nuestra señora de Zapopan) in the town of Zapopan, state of Jalisco built in the 17th century, many decades before Mexico declared independence from Spain in the year 1921. One of my wife's cousins picked us up at the airport and drove us over to the monastery. As we entered the ancient monastery I felt I was in colonial Mexico. As I walked through the wide hallways I noticed young men going about their daily chores. This monastery housed a seminary, filled with young Franciscan monks in their traditional robes singing and praying, laughing and learning.

Fray Kutchi's spiritual guide, a young, bearded, Franciscan Priest led us to a room along with other relatives that flew

in from the USA and drove from small towns around the
state of Jalisco. All of us standing around a tall coffee table
with a small backpack in the middle and its contents spread
around it. An extra shirt, a bible, three small prayer books,
three small notebooks, a comb, deodorant, rosary, several
address books, some torn or in pieces, and a pencil so small
you wonder how he could write with it and a pen without
ink.
"These are all of Fray's belongings" the Priest told us.
I turned to Gloria, "Imagine that, all of your life's
possessions fitting in this small backpack".

"I brought Fray down from the mountain" said the young
Priest. "He didn't want to come down but he was very
sick. Bury me here in the mountain he told me. I have to
bring you down to the monastery, you know that. I replied
to him. Ok said Fray, let me get my backpack I know I'm
not coming back".
I looked around to the crowd, they all were crying.
"Fray asked me to pray with him at night before he went to
sleep. The doctors gave him a lot of morphine as he was in
so much pain from dozens of tumors all over his stomach.
He told me he knew he wasn't going to wake up" said the
Priest.
We all stared at him hanging on his words without making
a sound.
"Did he say something before he closed his eyes?" I asked.
"Yes he did" said the Priest. "I'm so happy to be a Fray" he
said.

Thirty Times

The phone startled me. Ten thoughts crammed into my head before the second ring as my heart overreacted by hammering into my chest. It didn't ring differently, but it did. It rang in a way not expected, like when you get a call in the middle of the night, but it wasn't the middle of the night. It was a lazy Saturday morning, the type of morning where you're not expecting a call.

It was a day just like any other in San Diego, California. I live in a small city in the south of the county called Bonita, a quaint community where you chat with neighbors at Donny's, the local coffee shop. That day started as a proper Saturday should. You know, the usual plan. When you wake up and get up in the morning you always have a plan, or at least you know how things are going to go that day. Maybe you shower, eat something, go to work. Maybe you take the kids to the park and have some chores before lunch. Sometimes you think about what you have to do that day, or even specific tasks you need to accomplish. "I need to make some calls, send emails, pick up the kids, and go to the gym".

You don't know when something abnormal will happen, something you don't expect, an event that could change the tone of your day. Maybe it's someone you bump into from your past, maybe it's a natural event as a storm, or maybe it's a tragedy. This was one of these days.

The phone rang again. I picked up my cell. It was my aunt Lissette. "Hi Tia" I answered my phone. "Hello, your uncle Pepe is in the hospital", she said without any hesitation or explanation, not even preparation. "What happened?", I asked. "He was in an accident" She said. "Is he OK? I asked. "I don't know" she said. Her voice started trembling and I could hear her crying over the speaker.

"Is he alive?" I asked getting straight to the point.
"I don't know" she said.
"Where is he?" I asked. "The Red Cross in Tijuana" she said.
"How did you find out?" I asked.
"Your aunt Sonia called me from her house to tell me she received a call" she said, "she then left for the Red Cross but they would not give any information over the phone. That's all I know".

"How did they know to call her?" I asked.
"They found his cell phone on his pocket and decided to call every number on it until they got someone," she said.

I was taking deep breaths to stay calm. I knew he was at the Red Cross, he probably got into an accident, maybe a car accident. We did not have any other information. "I'll be right there to pick you up" I said. I lived just five minutes from my aunt's house so I could get there quickly. However, I remembered my wife was in Tijuana visiting her parents and the Red Cross was only ten minutes from their house. So, I quickly called her parent's house.

While I dialed, I thought what I would say and in what order. My wife answered the phone.

"Hello it's Jorge" I said.

"Hi, how are you?" she asked.

"I'm doing well. But my Uncle is at the Red Cross, we don't know what happened or how he got there. That's all we know; can you go right now?" I said.

"Yes I'll go immediately," she said, "Is he OK?"

"I don't know", I said, "We don't know anything else but we're on our way. I gave to go, please call me when you get there".

Gloria, my wife, was a bit shaken up but determined with the new task at hand. My wife didn't worry me. My aunt and my mother worried me. I feared for their health, for a heart attack or at the very least one of them fainting and hitting their head on the concrete.

I dialed my mother and could not find her anywhere. I called her house and her cell phone. No answer. I didn't leave a voice mail. I jumped in the car and picked up my aunt at her house. I was taking deep breaths through my nose and holding the air in as much as I could, then letting it go through my nose as slow as possible calming myself down. I had the shakes and I didn't want my aunt to see me trembling.

I could see my aunt as I approached her house from afar. She was out on the street waiting for me next to her driveway with a nervous stand. I made a U-turn and stopped in front of her. She got in the car on the passenger seat. She had a scary stare on her face. I leaned over to give her a kiss.

"Do you have your passport?" I asked her, noticing she didn't even reach for the seatbelt.

"What?" she said.

"Do you have your passport? You know you can't come back without your passport". I said smiling patiently.

"No, I could not find it" she said.

"Go back and look again" I said.

"I looked everywhere it's not there" she said.

"Take a deep breath" I told her looking at her straight in the eye. She closed her eyes and took a deep breath. "Now go get your passport" I told her. "Nothing will happen in the five minutes it will take you to look again".

She opened the door and went back into her house to look for her passport. At that moment the phone rang, I looked at the number, it was my wife.

"I'm at the Red Cross, your Aunt Sonia is here," she said quickly. "Your uncle was stabbed at least thirty times and is in surgery right now".

"Did you speak with the doctors?" I asked.

"No, there are many policeman here and they don't let us in. The lobby is as far as we can go." she said,

"We can't see him, speak with anyone, that's what the receptionist told us".

"OK we're on our way I'm picking up Aunt Lissette." I said.

"What about your mother?" she asked.

"Only voice mail. I'll go to her house to see if she's there".

I called my mother again and this time she answered.

"Bueno?", she answered.

"Mother how are you?" I said in Spanish.

"I'm good son, how are you?", she said as she always says.

"Mom, are you at your house?" "Yes I'm here" she answered.

"Good, I will pick you up in fifteen minutes, I'm already in the car" I said, "Uncle Pepe got into a car accident and is in the Red Cross in Tijuana" I lied. I could not say "Your brother got stabbed thirty times". I figured I would tell her once she was in the car with her sister.

At this point, less than one hour passed since I received the first phone call. I forgot what I needed to do that morning, or that day, or that week. I forgot if I had a job, or kids, or responsibilities. I had already prayed at least 30 Hail

Mary's and was mumbling them back to back even while on the phone. I was also mumbling "please help my uncle, please help my uncle, please help my uncle" over and over again. I was worried about my aunt and how confused she looked before I sent her back for her passport. I was still worried about my mother and how she would react. We didn't even mention anything to my grandmother. She lost her other two sons when they were in their twenties, she would not survive another tragedy.

In those minutes, everything that matters in the world came to the front of my mind and stayed there implanted like a tattoo on my forehead, everything that's trivial was gone. Even things that I thought were important before, or that I had to urgently get done that day. Nothing mattered at that moment except for my family. It's interesting what tragedy does to the brain and how it reacts. In this case, my brain tried to push emotions aside and get into problem solving mode. "Don't be nervous, don't overreact, take care of your aunt and your mother" my brain barked orders. I obeyed each one of them.

My aunt returned with her passport in hand. "It was in the nightstand" she said with a shrug of the shoulders. "I never leave it there" she said.
"Good" I said. And explained how her brother was stabbed but alive. "Take a deep breath through your nose" I told her. She did, several. Her stare was blank forward. "Put your seat belt on" I had to remind her.

"I told my mother Pepe got into a car accident" I said. Lissette had a blank stare.

"Oh, alright" she said snapping back into the car from wherever her mind was. "Good idea, let's tell her when she's in the car" she said.

"Yes, and let's tell her he's alive first so that we don't let her panic" I said. We drove a short while towards my mother's house. She saw the car outside and exited her condo to get in the car behind me.

"Hello mother" I said.

"Hello son" she responded. Our usual greeting. "Hello sister" my mom told my aunt. Before she asked any questions, I told my mom "Pepe is alive but he did not get into a car accident, he got stabbed".

I looked back and so did my aunt. My mom had seemed to have a mask on her face, one I could only describe as a mask of terror. She stopped breathing.

"Rosa!" my aunt told her form her front seat bending at her waist. "Rosa" she repeated raising her voice, "Breathe, he's OK, we told you he's ok" she said.

My mom took a gasp and looked at my aunt, then me, then my aunt again, her mouth trembling, eyes watery and face pale.

"Mom, we're on our way, we know he's alive and that's what counts". She nodded.

I drove south towards the San Diego border as calm as one can drive under the circumstances. Trying to keep my passengers calm and concentrated on the task at hand. I glanced at my cell phone when I could while keeping enough concentration on the road. Trying to make it ring with good news. No phone call came, no good news. We crossed the border through the San Ysidro check point. After tackling the busiest border crossing in the world, we continued east towards my old stomping grounds. We parked a block away from the Red Cross and saw a coffee shop.

"I'll come back for some coffee after" I said.

As the three of us walked in, we saw Gloria, my Aunt Sonia and her husband Miguel sitting in the tiny waiting area. I would not even call it a lobby. It had five chairs and nothing else. No table, no vending machine, nothing. The place felt cold in more ways than one. The floor was cold, the walls looked cold, and the people felt cold.

"All we know is that he's out of surgery and he'll survive" said my Aunt Sonia as soon as we walked in.
Everyone hugged a long hug, even by our standards.
"He got stabbed at least thirty times, the doctors don't know how he made it" said Uncle Miguel shaking his head.
"Did you go in to see him?" asked my Aunt Lissette.
"No, they don't let anyone it, it's a high security area, especially since it was a violent crime" said Aunt Sonia.
We all stood looking at each other, my mom walked over to the door to plea her case to the guard and receptionist sitting behind a bullet proof window in a box like booth.

"Nobody can go in" both the receptionist and the police officer carrying a shotgun said.

My mom walked six paces back to us "Nobody can go in" she told us.

We asked Aunt Sonia, the first on the scene, every question we could think off. "How did you find out? When did you get here? Who's the doctor?" and many more. She answered every question more than once with patience. We then made sure the entire family knew of what happened by calling each of them on our cell phones. It only took a few calls as we asked them to call everyone else.

"Ask who can spend the night here" asked my Aunt Sonia when she called one of her nephews.

One hour passed and then two. We asked to go in whenever we saw a new face exit the hospital. We were denied every time. It was time to eat now and we went to get food, then coffee, hours passed and we got more coffee. No news came from inside. My mom was now mad and about to go and scream at the receptionist. I could see it in her face. This is uncharacteristic of her but I can see how having your brother dying in the next room can persuade you to scream at a receptionist.

"Mom, calm down" I said before she stood up glaring at the receptionist booth. "This is the place they bring victims of violent crimes as well as injured criminals from the cartel. This is why they're paranoid about security". She looked around and saw other armored police stationed outside the hospital. She then sat back down.

We passed the time telling stories about Uncle Pepe. My Aunt Sonia was knitting, my mom and Aunt Lissette called their husbands every fifteen minutes with status reports, "Nothing new" they reported. Chatting calmed our anxiety, everyone there is an extraordinary conversationalist and time didn't stale. Humor pierced every topic, even in such opaque situations we managed to laugh at life and ourselves. It seemed to me we didn't even take death very seriously.

A recognizable figure appeared out of the corner of my eye entering the small hospital. I turned and affixed by stare at the figure trying to recognize him. There was something familiar to his walk, or his profile, or something I can't describe. I turned to look at my mother and she was doing the same. Squinting to as if that would augment her eyesight or as if to turn on her recognition software. The man continued walking towards the door behind the reception cube. I could clearly hear the steps of his black dress shoes clinking on the cheap tile floor smelling of disinfectant. Our glare was too heavy on him and he felt it, turning cautiously as if we had called him to do so. He glared at me and then at my mother, our concentrated stares crossed once and twice. He had recognition in his eyes. The man, probably a doctor, stopped and blinked hard for half a second as if that would give him the answer he looked for. I stood up slowly and closed the distance between us with short steps. "Luis?" I asked. "Jorge?" He responded, a soft tingle parked on my neck.

"What are you doing here?" he said while standing his hand. I shook his hand and hugged my long-lost friend. He used to be my neighbor and playmate when we were eleven years old. Apparently now he was a doctor. "Do you remember my mother?" I said, she was already next to me arms extended asking for a hug "Luisito how are you?" she said.

"What are you doing here?" I asked.
"I'm here to see a patient, I'm a pediatric surgeon" he said looking at me and then back at my mother.
She stood up and joined us in recognition. We explained our situation and how we could not go inside the hospital gates.
"Follow me" he said as he walked in passed the secured door as if he owned the place, me in pursuit before somebody changed their mind. We continued walking through the emergency door used for ambulances and through a door. It was the supply room crowded by doctors and nurses in uniform.

"Give me a second" he said raising his index figure.
He stepped away speaking with a nurse and a young man in a light gray lab coat. Much too young to be a doctor. Luis came back with him. "Your uncle is stable" the young man

said. He looked to be twenty-four years old. Short, baby faced with too much styling gel in his hair. "He was stabbed over thirty times from his head all the way to his stomach including close to his heart, lung, eyes, and skull, everywhere. Half of the stabs came a centimeter or two from a vital organ. I'm not sure how he's still alive" the young man shrugged. "I guess it was not his time. We see everything here in this hospital and sometimes we just can't explain it. This is one of those times". He said.

I smiled faintly in relief. "Some good news" I said exhaling, not knowing if I should smile or not.

"I'll be back in an hour" said the young man, he shook my hand and left.

"Who was that?" I asked Luis once the young man exited and closed the door behind him.

"That was the head surgeon" he said.

"What? He looks like he's in high school" I said.

Luis smirked remembering my sense of humor long forgotten.

"Oh no, he's very experienced" he said. "He does surgeries all day every day: stabbings, car accidents, shootings, he's like a battlefield doctor" he said.

I nodded in surprise while looking around at the room mostly empty.

"This is the supply room" said Luis.

"Not much of a supply room" I said.

Luis took a step towards one of five cabinets and opened it. Ten syringes and five bandages adorned one of the shelves. The other two shelves had nothing.

"Wow, how do they manage?" I asked.

"Mostly volunteers like me and donations" he said.

This is one of the times you get the feeling you're spoiled. I probably had more supplies in my emergency kit than they did in their supply room.

"Follow me" said Luis walking out of the supply room a few paces towards a large curtain acting as a door. Luis pulled the curtain to reveal a large room with six beds in a row one next to each other standing in the middle of the rectangular room. I spied my uncle on the penultimate bed staring at the wall, eyes open in contemplation. I pointed at him.

"There he is" I told Luis.

He walked me over to his bed and spoke to the nurse in charge. "He's my good friend, please let him stay as long as he and his family wants" he told them. "I have to go see my patient" he told me. "I'll be back soon".

I smiled as I approached my uncle's bed. He smiled with his mouth closed, his trademark smile. "What's up dude?" I asked and nodded in a manly way. His entire face was covered with stitches from the top of his head to his neck. All knife wounds from earlier that morning. I've never seen or even imagined anything like it. Not in books, not in movies, it was too gruesome to see but I forced to look without flinching. "What's up?" he responded and nodded back. "Not your best day" I said. He laughed loudly as I embraced him with a hug and kissed his forehead. Small and large stitches scratched his forearms, shoulder, face, ears and throat. With longer stitches protruding from his fingers and both of his palms. I couldn't see his chest as it was covered with a blanket.

"All your sisters are outside" I told him. I said while running my finger through one of his scars.
"Your kids are on their way".
"Good" he said nodding and grinning.
"We've been here since this morning but they didn't let us in" I explained. I didn't want him to think he was alone. Everyone was there, praying for him. I wasn't sure what you should say or if it was prudent to ask what happened. He didn't look in shock or drugged. He looked fine.

"My neighbor's construction worker knocked on my kitchen door" he started. "He asked me for something to eat, he looked hungry. When I turned back into the kitchen to get something for him he took a knife from the table and stabbed me in the back right here" he pointed towards the back of his right shoulder.

I said nothing. Uncle Pepe took a deep breath and nodded several times in his usual way.
"My legs gave out as I dropped to my knees and then my stomach with a rush of pain raining on me. I felt him

coming for me and managed to turn on my back to face him. I ordered my legs to lift and kick him back but they didn't listen. He landed on me, sitting on my stomach and legs beside my ribs, and raised his arm atop his head while holding my neck with his other hand. The fist and knife came down as a punch into my heart as I scratched his face with one hand and tried to remove the other from my wind pipe. I felt the blade go all the way in, saw it go out painted red. I screamed at him and went for his eyes but couldn't reach. He repeated his motion raising his fist and striking down time and time again. I couldn't harm him, so I tried to stop the blows with my hands and forearms. I managed to stop the ones on my chest, so he targeted my face." he lifted his forearms so I could see the cost of stopping the knife.

"I managed to grab his knife by the blade a few times but he pulled it out ripping my hands open".
He extended his hands to show me both his palms made into a crazy pattern of stitches that popped out of his hands creating a new dimension. I nodded following the story and sat on his bed.
"After his efforts failed to kill me by stabbing my stomach and chest, he was determined to stick the knife into my left eye".
You could see all the small stitches around his eye as the tip of the knife hit his hard skull without penetrating.

"It seemed like I was fighting him off for six hours" said
Uncle Pepe staring at me.

I looked around. There were two armed guards next to me
guarding the patient in the next bed only nine or ten feet
away. They wore heavy bullet proof vests. One had a
shotgun and the other an AK 47.

"Who's that guy?" I asked my uncle.

"He's a drug trafficker" he answered in a whisper. "He got
shot in a raid and all the security you see here is because
they expect the other gang to come and finish him off". He
said.

"Oh great" I thought. That's all we need. A platoon of
armed traffickers to come in and start shooting people. But
I just nodded in acknowledgement.

The nurse came to check on my uncle.

"You're busy" I told the nurse.

"Oh yes," she said with a tired voice and very tired eyes.
She didn't say it, but I knew she was probably working
overtime and had to do it with little to no supplies. She
pealed down the blanket covering my uncle and revealed
his chest and stomach. His stomach was covered with the
bandages wrapped several times around his entire stomach.
His chest looked like what you would expect to see from a
medieval torture session in a hidden, damp, dark dungeon.
I could see where the killer tried to stab the heart time and
time again, and where the doctors performed surgery to
patch up the insides that where on the outside when he first
made his way into the emergency room.

She finishing checking his bandages and gauze; then changed his IV drip before leaving. I was happy that my uncle survived and grateful the Red Cross was here to save his life. I also felt a mixture of shame and hopelessness of having my uncle in this environment. It looked lacking, simple, underequipped and not suited for the job. "I want more for my uncle" I thought. "He deserves much more than this".

Being conscious of the time, I knew I had to go back to the lobby and let his sisters in, but I decided to ask for the entire story before I exited.
"How did you survive?" I prompted him to continue where he left off.
"I knew I was fighting for my life." He continued. "I saw my eyes going black several times and mustered energy to stay awake, to stay alive. I knew if I closed my eyes I was dead. I wasn't fighting for my wallet; I was fighting for my life. One or two minutes more would determine if I was dead or alive. I decided to live" he said.
He looked at me. His eyes come as if he was describing a book or a movie. I was much more nervous and anxious than he was.

"After I decided I wanted to live I continued trying to catch the blade of the knife with my hand and break it. It slipped from my grasp several times, my hand cut to shreds and slippery with blood coming down my forearms and splattering my face. It was now hard to see and the blade kept escaping time and time again, further cutting my hand and fingers". He paused and looked up as if remembering what happened next.

"Finally I trapped the knife and twisted my wrist to detach the blade form the wooden handle" he continued. "He immediately stood up unarmed looking for another knife or something to use as a weapon. I don't know how I did it but I stood up in half a second, blood soaking my clothes and slipping on my own blood on the kitchen floor I almost fell down. I managed to take the nearest chair and used it as a barrier. I held it up in front of me. He grabbed it and pulled it hard. I held it pulling back all my remaining strength for only a few seconds while screaming profanities at him to hoping he would think I held some strength. It worked. When he realized he had no chance, he finally let go of the chair and ran out. Just like that it was over. Now I needed to get help" he said.

My uncle lives in the house I grew up in. It's out in a remote area of the city with only three houses as neighbors. To get to the nearest house my uncle needed to exit through the kitchen door, go up a flight of twenty steep steps and cross the street.

"How did you get out of the house?" I asked.

Uncle Pepe took a small sip of water from a cardboard cup he held with his right hand atop his leg. "As soon as my attacker left, I dropped the chair and thought about lying down on the cement kitchen floor. I was soaked in blood as if I took a shower in it. My left knee fell to the grown without my permission. Stand Up, Stand Up I commanded. Maybe the man would come back, or maybe if I stopped to rest fatigue would have me and I would never wake up. I tried to stand up and my left leg was paralyzed. I leaned against the refrigerator and pushed on the chair to stand up. Then I used the refrigerator, the stove, and the wall to sustain me while I reached the door. It was open so I rested with my back to the door and mustered all the energy I could into one long scream: Help!

I had at least ten questions but didn't want to interrupt. Dread covered my throat and it felt dry. I could hear the moans of the other patients. Some shot, some recovering from accidents or emergency surgery.

"The scream zapped all the energy I had. I looked up the stairs to take measure, an impossible climb. Maybe that was the end. As I looked up again, I saw the head of my neighbor pop up to find me. He saw me drenched in red and almost leaped all the way down the stairs to help me".

"Oh my god Pepe, what happened? He asked in horror, not knowing if he should even touch me, I was holding my stomach with my left hand preventing my insides from pushing out of my body. I could feel their gravity pushing against my hand."

"Take me to the hospital, I was attacked" I told him, ready to pass out in pain and loss of blood.
He hesitated before taking my right arm and swinging it over his shoulder and helping me up the stairs. He carried me more than anything else. I passed out right before reaching his car for one or two seconds. Then passed out again when he put me in the back seat".

I shook my head and gathered my wit. "The doctor told me you're out of danger" I told him. I didn't ask my questions about the attack. "Te quiero Tio Pepe (I love you uncle Pepe)" I told him. Kissed his forehead and left to get his sisters.

After my mother and aunts went in and out to see him, I told them I would go to uncle Pepe's house to get him clean clothes. All the ones he came with ended up in the trash. From shirt to socks, shoes, everything.
"Get him toothpaste, toothbrush, deodorant and hand lotion" said Aunt Sonia. His hands were rasp and they didn't have any lotion here.
"I'll go with you" said my wife.
"Me too" my mother got up and grabbed her purse.

We drove the short distance from the Red Cross to my Uncle's place. I parked and turned to my wife and my mother.

"Wait here" I'll tell you when to come down.

"Why?" asked my mother.

"Mom, the attacker might be in the house, and I want to survey the kitchen before you go in. Lock the doors" I said while I exited the car.

As I walked down the cement steps I prepared myself to see blood. The door was opened. I pushed it all the way. I saw horror.

Not knowing how to process the scene I started praying in my native Spanish "Padre nuestro que estas en el cielo (Our father who are in heaven)". I was much worse than what I imagined and prepared for. It was not just the blood splatter on the table, chairs and appliances. A carafe of water broke with the struggle and it covered the entire kitchen floor with red. It looked like more than a gallon of blood was covering every inch of the kitchen floor. I knew it was blood mixed with water but had to warn my mother and Gloria before they entered. The entire kitchen had one long strip of blood where my uncle leaned to make it all the way to the door. It looked like someone took a wide paintbrush and painted the stripe from one side of the kitchen to the other going over appliances in their way.

I took photos in case the police asked me for a report and went back up the stairs to fetch them.

"The floor and the wall is covered with blood" I told them. There are broken plates and glasses so be careful. Prepare yourselves before you go in" I said.

My warnings did not help my mother. She almost fainted as I saw her legs buckle. "Mom" I screamed at her to try and get their attention and snap her out of it. She looked at me, her hand trembling covering her mouth. It was a crime scene. Nothing like you see in the movies. The scene was splattered with blood and gore. The refrigerator had large circular stain from when Pepe leaned into it to stand up. The stove had been sprayed with blood in the front and had several large stains on top. The table was bloody, the wall, and drops of dried blood covered everything, from the corner to the plates drying on the sink, even the ceiling.

"Do you want to go outside?" I asked my mother.

She stared at me and shook her head snapping out of it.

"No, sorry, I'm fine, it's just this is…" she was at a loss for words.

"I know" I said. "Let's go to his bedroom to find his clothes."

After we picked clothes for my uncle and delivered them to the Red Cross we headed back home to San Diego. My cousin Gabriel stayed the night with him.

"What a day" I told everyone before leaving the hospital.

"At least everything is stable now" said my uncle Miguel.

They all nodded in approval and headed to their respected homes.

Although emotionally exhausted it was hard to fall asleep. My mind kept going back to my uncle, his scars, the operation he endured and the scene of gore that was in his kitchen. I woke up in the morning not knowing how much I slept. I felt tired and my eyes had a dark half-moon resting under it.

I got a call early. I know it was another bad one.
"One of his lungs was punctured and it's leaking fluid and he's going to the operation room right now" said my Uncle Miguel.
I closed my eyes and started praying again. "Dios te salve, Reina y Madre".
After waking up Gloria and taking a very quick shower, we picked up my mother and Aunt Lissette again, praying all the way to the hospital.

As we arrived back at the Tijuana Red Cross, he was out of surgery.
"We initially missed this puncture wound but it's now stitched" said the surgeon. The same baby faced young man as the day before.
My cousin Miguel was there before I arrived. He lives two miles from my house in San Diego. "We need to take him to the US" I told him.

Miguel organized the delivery of the uncle to the international border. Uncle Pepe's son and daughter organized the pick up from the US ambulance on the other side.

As we arrived at the US hospital in Hillcrest, near downtown San Diego, the doctor was checking on his status.

"They did an amazing job" the doctor told us. "It looks like a master surgeon" he said.

"It was a kid that looked twelve years old" I told the doctor. "But he operates all day long so he has the experience" I told him.

"This man should be dead" he told me seriously. "Not once, but several times over. It is as if something blocked the knife from hitting his heart, his eyes, and his lungs. The knife took weird angles to avoid the target." The doctor said.

"My uncle has a gigantic guardian angel" I told the doctor with a smile.

"Well, your explanation is better than mine" he said shrugging his shoulders.

It was a happy ending. All the family was there in San Diego at the hospital joking with him and making him laugh. I stepped out of the room into the hallway to cry by myself. Finally releasing my jaw, my back muscles, and my mind from a grip that I can't explain. I cried for ten minutes before I went back into his room and joined the family.

Giving thanks to my uncle's Guardian Angel for giving my uncle a second, third, and fourth chance at life, and giving us the opportunity to love him many years longer.

Lesson: Wake-Up Calls

Imagine you stayed in a hotel during a trip and have to get up early to take a flight home. You don't trust your phone to wake you up. "What if I don't wake up with the alarm?" you think. "I'll miss my plane and that would be bad, very bad". You walk over to your hotel room phone and dial zero. "Could I get a wake-up call?" you tell the person on the other side. What does this mean? It means you would like an interruption to your slumber. You need a third party to interfere with your sleep and wake you up. This is the literal definition of a wake-up call. We all heard it before. The analogy is when we apply it to life. When someone gets sick or in an accident "It was a wake-up call and now I'll take care of myself and spend more time with my family". It is a life-stopping moment that either hurdles you in another direction or reminds you what's important in your life: People. Nobody says: "I will now put in more overtime" after having a wake-up call.

That day with my uncle has not been my first or last wake-up call. This is why I try to live everyday with the same attitude I had in those crucial moments. That day I didn't remember anything about checking email, or voice mail, or anything else. I just wanted my uncle to survive and for my mom, my aunts and my family to feel normal. To feel hope, happiness, and to stop the sorrow and the hopelessness they felt.

Life stops our forward momentum in different ways. It may be God tugging at your elbow to get your attention, or destiny remembering you what you're supposed to be doing, or what you're supposed to hold dear and valuable. You may call it a wake-up call, others a new opportunity. Whatever it is. Don't wait for a heart attack to change your life. Don't wait for a life changing event. Treat every morning as a life changing event. When you get up in the morning realize it's not your right to wake up. Don't expect it. Treat it as a surprise party, as something you received whether you deserve it or not. Wake up to a surprise party where all your friends congratulate you, hug you and tell you they love you. That's what waking up should feel like.

Once you wake up, work towards deserving the next day. Treat everyone as if they're the most important person in the world. Especially the poor, the subordinates and the ones you just used to give no more than a glance before. It's easy to treat the queen as a queen, to be polite towards your boss or the billionaire you met on a conference. It is much more difficult to treat the cleaning lady as the queen. How do you know she's not? Work today as if you have to win tomorrow. What would you do if there was a test? Depending on how you treat others will depend on if you wake up. What would you do? How would you treat your spouse, family, friends and most especially the ones you don't know?

Work each day towards waking up tomorrow. It's not about working hard at the office, or with the kids, or giving to charity. It's about how you look people in the eye and transmit respect, care, and love. It's about listening before speaking, about putting the needs of others before yours. Work every day towards deserving to wake up the next, because one day, you won't.

The Science of Everything

It was day like any other at my school in Tijuana, Mexico. A private catholic school called Instituto Mexico, a Marian school run by Marists, monk like teachers dedicating their life to the Virgin Mary and to education of our youth. I was in my classroom sitting all the way in the back-right corner looking outside, as usual, instead of looking at the teacher. There was nothing to see as everyone was in class. However, the stillness was more interesting than my teacher.

My friend Javier strolled by the open corridor and saw me daydreaming from inside the small, long rectangular window. He stopped for two seconds and laughed.

"Pay attention" he whispered to me coming close to the window.

I laughed with him. He's also a day dreamer, an incredible storyteller even at that early age. He had his oversized wooden cross hanging from a string around his neck. A beautiful handmade cross he got from his missionary trip to the mountains in Chihuahua visiting the Tarahumara Indians.

I wanted to go with him. I had decided one year previous I would be a missionary, but I wasn't able to go and missed his incredible adventure. My mother didn't let me go. "Your education is the most important thing in your life" she had told me. "Finish your university and then you can do whatever you want".

This was not the first time I heard this. It was an ongoing mantra since I was six or seven years of age. I think this is a good time to clarify something. My mother is a religious woman. Not just in the general, going to church or reading the bible kind of religious. She's a scholar. My mother graduated from the catholic seminary with all priests on her generation, except for her. Yes, the only non-priest and the only woman in her class, the only woman in that seminary school to ever graduate. I had theology, philosophy and literature as communion every single day. She was a teacher on the subject and I was one of her pupils since the day she entered the seminary. Even with that mystical education, she felt that my traditional schooling was more important than whatever a mission in the mountains could bring.

Even though leaving my home and my friends in exchange for the mountains was what I wanted, I did not do it. I honored my mother's wishes as it is tradition in matriarchal Mexican families such as my own. I stayed in school and didn't even go to the missions in the summer. But it bothered me. I felt a calling to the mountains, or at least to help those who are the least helped. The Marist taught us not only to pray or to praise God. That was not their way, their way was to work. Yes, to get your hands dirty and plow, hammer, educate, and make a social difference. "You can hammer and pray at the same time" was one of my favorite sayings.

Even though I stayed in school and wasn't a missionary working in remote places around the world, I was what I could only describe as a part time missionary. We had an apostolic group in the school that I joined in junior high and it soon became one of the central activities of my life. We worked on the weekends and learned, prayed and socialized together during the week. We continued this good habit long after high school and into our college years.

Looking out of that window, looking at my friend's cross was a pivotal moment in my life. I didn't know then that taking or not taking that path in that single moment would change my life. Not better or worse, just different. But I could not let it go. I felt an emptiness in my heart for not serving humanity. An emptiness that my friend's beautifully carved cross reminded me every day and every time I saw him. I couldn't shake it; I was obsessed with it. My ideologies mixed with my teenage passion to make the moment even more unbearable. It was so bad I dreamt of having a wooden cross hanging across my neck for three straight nights. I never told anyone about this before until now. Not about my dreams for three straight nights, not about my desire to be a missionary.

The bell rang and brought me out of my trance. We had a couple of minutes before our next class to stretch our legs. The next teacher came in, we prayed a Holy Mary and he started with his lecture on Calculus. It took five minutes to go back into the business of looking out the window and daydreaming. After class, we had a fifteen minute break. I usually spent every minute of every day playing basketball. This day I decided to go to the school chapel to chat a bit and sit with down God for fifteen minutes. I always felt special when I walked out of that chapel, it had an enchanting quality about it. It was not what you would expect to find in a Catholic chapel. It was an old classroom with wall to wall carpeting and no chairs and no windows. It had no light but a few candles at the front next to a small cross and an image if the Virgin Mary of Guadalupe. Visitors kneeled on the wooden stools rising only six to eight inches from the floor remnant of meditating monks. It was what you expect to find at a Buddhist monastery not necessarily a catholic chapel.

I entered and kneeled monk stile for a few minutes emptying my mind and concentrating on god. A few moments later, my friend Vianett entered with her guitar. She used to go several times per week to sing. She had a sweet melodious voice that always made me cry. That day was not an exception. I stayed there until I had to get up and go back to class. I smiled at her and she smiled back without missing a note on her acoustic guitar. I always wondered if she carried the thing from her house on a daily basis.

As I exited the chapel back to the playground in the middle of the school, I remembered my dream and held my chest as if looking for my cross. I smiled feeling ridiculous and walked away looking around for staring faces. As I strolled back to the middle of the playground I heard someone call my name almost in a whisper, "Olson" I heard. I turned back to see Bruno, one of my teachers and a theology scholar as well as a veteran Marist. I always considered him a literary character straight out of one of my stories, thick beard half filled with gray, he seemed to know everything about philosophy, theology and literature. He resembled a penguin moving side to side while walking in his slow methodical way. If you had a question, no matter how specific or obscure, you knew where to go. His character could surely be an owl and a wizard all in one. Professor Bruno was always very quiet and deliberate, looking at you from atop his glasses with his head down he always dressed the same. As with many Marist, he probably only had two sets of clothes.

As I turned toward my teacher he waved me over with his hand. I walked the way I came and up the chapel steps. "Yes sir" I said after a second of silence. He said nothing, looking at me over his glasses he stretched his left hand; it was closed palm facing down. "This is unusual" I thought as I looked at his still hand for half a second, then followed it up to meet his eyes for another half a second as they held no expression. He blinked and moved his hand in a small shake inviting me to take whatever contents it had. I reluctantly raised my right hand looking very confused at this game and opened it under his hand my palm facing up. He opened his hand to place a wooden cross upon my hand. It was a hand carved cross with a string to place it around my neck. I looked up with what I could only imagine where tearful confused eyes. A rush of emotion falling over me, hitting my nervous system like an adrenaline shot.

"I know you've been dreaming about this cross" He told me, and walked away.

Five tears dove to the pavement disappearing into the ground. I didn't even feel them touch my cheeks. I held the cross on my hand and placed it over my chest letting out a breath that I was probably holding in for a while. It felt good to breathe. I looked up to see Bruno walking away. I took two steps after him to ask a million questions about what happened, how did he know, who gave him the cross, how much did he know about... he turned back as if on cue and stopped my forward motion by raising his old hand. "You can't know everything. There are things you just don't understand" he told me.

I was sixteen years old at the time, and since then I've studied as much as I can. Not only religious studies of every kind but history, economy science and everything an aspiring polymath would study. I would like to say I studied the science of everything. Socrates was correct as well as old Professor Bruno was as well. There are things I just don't understand.

The Lesson of Perseverance

"Buenas Tardes" I said while pointing at the picture of the clock in the Spanish book.

"Buenas Tardes" my student repeated with a heavy English-American accent. It was my second class of the day. I was teaching Spanish as a second language over at a prominent language school in San Diego, CA. My other class that day was Doing Business in English. I liked both classes, but I was partial to Spanish as it's my mother language and one of the most romantic, most expressive languages in the world, if I do say so myself. I didn't realize I would be teaching business geniuses for ten bucks an hour, but that was the gig. What can a young kid from Tijuana teach giants of industry? Absolutely nothing! At least nothing about business.

After I graduated from San Diego State University I thought I would be entry level something or other, then senior something, after this, maybe manager in a few months, then director in a year, Vice President, Sr. Vice President... you get the drift. I needed to make money and help my family back in Mexico. My goals were simple:

electricity, paved roads and running water, just not in the living room, so I had to fix the leaking roof.

To my surprise nobody wanted to hire me. I mean nobody. I could not get an interview with the receptionist to try and sell myself to get an interview with the HR or hiring manager. I didn't understand. I was going to work twelve hours per day and making my boss famous. My goals were not going according to, well, to plan.

After sixty days without landing a full-time gig, I was applying to every job I could find in the newspaper not just what I thought I wanted. I received a call back from a language school. "I'll take the job, whatever hours" I told them. Now I was working around three hours per day three days per week making ten dollars per hour; around one or one and a half minimum wage at the time. Now let me tell you the rest of the story, the semi-dramatic part. I lived in Tijuana, across the border from San Diego, in Mexico. The border wait to cross into the USA ranged from one hour to two hours per day. It took me at least two hours to get to work and at least one hour to get back. Yes, I drove three hours to work... three hours! Hey! It paid the gas. I also discovered audio books at the time and I could go through a book per day, or one every two days just on my commute.

As an eternal optimist, I thought something good would happen from this job, or from any job. The CEO of the company would come from headquarters and ask "who is this hard working young man?" be impressed with me and hire me as his vice president of global operations. Nope, that didn't happen. I kept applying for every single job that I could find, well, except for a doctor, engineer or lawyer. I'm not "Pretender" for those of you who remember the TV show. Didn't get a single email, call, letter, fax, telegram, smoke signal or job offer; so, I continued to wait in line at the border to cross and get to my job. Was this the wonderful world of employment that awaited me? Part time hours wherever I could find them? What about the full time executive corner office dream? Was that only for the well-connected or rich kids?

My fellow teachers were all older, much older, two or three times older than me. They all had an air of sophistication and knowledge. They looked like, mmm, how can I put it? Like smart people. The one thing I noticed really quickly is that they didn't make friends. They were not really friends with me or the other teachers and certainly not with the students. Don't get me wrong. They were very polite and well managed. But they were not making friends. Not going out for a beer or anything like that. I thought that was really weird. After all, these students came from France, Spain, Holland, China, Korea, and all over the world to San Diego to study English. And I later discovered how they played golf and enjoyed the sunshine on their company's budget. It was a great destination to spend one or two months with the pretext of learning to do business in English. Not a bad idea.

My gig was easy. "How to do business in English" was a breeze to teach. Fifty minutes of one-on-one private conversation about business. I decided I would turn this opportunity into my MBA. My first student entered the small room. I had three chairs, a small round table and my open book sitting atop. Nothing else, no distractions.

"Hello, my name is Jorge Olson, I will be your instructor" I said.
He introduced himself and sat down in one of the chairs. He had a thick French accent, was around sixty years old with fifty percent gray hair dressed in what looked to be an expensive long sleeve shirt and a blue sport coat.
"The best way of learning how to do business in English is to actually do it" I told him. "Our classes will be exactly that. You will describe everything you do for me and I will ask questions along the way".
"That is good" He said in a serious tone while nodding.
"What do you do in your job?" I asked him.
"I'm the President of Deloitte" he said.
I didn't know what that was.

This is how I started my higher education. Sure, I was going through a book on tape every other day on my commute, but this was different. This was a one-on-one mentoring session with an executive. I had a semester to go to finish my MBA at the university but decided not to enroll. My faith was in this new way of learning.

"Tell me what you do" I asked my next student. "I'm the CEO of one of the largest software firms in the world" he said.

"Score!" I thought.

That summer I had incredible students. Some of the top international firms sent their managers and employees to learn English at the school, and I was at the front lines. I had students from all over the world working for governments, medium companies and very large corporations. I thought this was an incredible place to meet interesting people. What I found odd was that my fellow teachers did not establish relationships with any of the students. Sure, they said hello to everyone. But I took them out for coffee, invited them for dinner and took them around San Diego to see the city. After all, they're visiting from another country; we have to be an example.

What I really wanted to do is take everyone to Tijuana and show them the city. Not all wanted to go, but most did. We ate Mexican food at my favorite places, toured the city, visited local pubs and engaged in terrific, international conversation. Oh such good times! This hospitality was normal for me. If you have a guest you show them around, take them shopping, introduce them to all your friends and make sure they have the best time possible. I could never understand why the other teachers didn't do the same. I thought everyone was hospitable. I was wrong.

I didn't learn everything about relationships from my Guardian Angel. Yes, I learned lots, but before we get into that, let me tell you how I learned about relationships from my mother and my grandmother. You see, I grew up with them, both hard working women that worked more than twelve hours per day. But they both had a lot of friends. Now when I mean a lot, I don't mean five or ten, or even twenty or thirty. I thought that everyone in the entire city was their friend at one point in time as a child. Imagine walking into your local restaurant and not being able to sit down at your table to eat lunch because you have to stop at every table and say hello to everyone. That was them. I later discovered at least one of the reasons. My grandmother sold business cards and other printing services door to door form one business to the next. She walked the entire city and sat down with every single small business owner to get to know them their family, kids, dreams, basically everything about the individual. They all loved her, and she sold some business cards. Can you imagine? My grandma was a door to door saleswoman. And she did it in high heels!

Her sensibility towards people was highly developed. I'm sure it was practiced and learned from years of sitting down with hundreds of customers and friends. Not necessarily genetic. In fact, I can tell you I've practiced my own relationship skills for hundreds of hours. How to be a better husband, son, cousin, friend, boss and salesperson. You name it, I've studied it, practiced it and tested it. You're not born with it. You have to work at it.

My mother has the same emotional intelligence multiplied by ten. That reminds me of one Friday afternoon that I drove to the gas station we used for the business. This is where all my drivers gassed up before going on their route in a family business we operated some years back. I got out of the car and walk into the store attached to the gas station. "Good afternoon. I'll fill up my tank. Account 11409" I said.

As I was walking out of the store the clerk called "Wait, who are you? I don't think I have you on my list".

I stopped, and walked back to the counter.

"I'm Jorge, I'm the owner".

He looked at me suspiciously for a moment. "Ah, Jorge, you're Rosa's son, right?" He said.

I thought for a moment on how he could know that. Then I remember who my mother was and how she makes friends.

"Yes I am" I responded. His face lit up.

"Oh my god, you are so lucky" he said. "Please tell your Mom I took her advice. I fixed the problems with my son, got back to school and stopped drinking." he said with a proud smile over his tanned face.

I clucked. Typical Mom, she probably walked into the gas station and found out his entire life. After a few tanks of gas, she was an influencer, a friend, and a mentor.

"I sure will" I said as I smiled. I shook his hand to properly introduce myself and walked out.

"Wait" he said. "Would you like some coffee before you go? It's on me".

It's easy for my mother to make friends and everyone I meet that realizes she's my mom tells me the same thing. "Oh my god you're Rosa's son. You are so lucky. We love Rosa". Yeah, yeah, yeah. I've heard it a hundred times. No, just kidding. I'm very proud every time I hear it. It makes me smile and I usually answer. "I know, I know". If I would have to tell you the one thing that makes me feel that my mother stands out and be a relationship magnet, it would be that she cares. She cuts all the bull shit, all the fluff, and she simply wants to know about you. Not your business, your job or the weather, about you.

One of my students was a friendly looking German who came to school with his assistant, or secretary, or colleague. "She's my boss" he would say but clearly she was a subordinate. I later found out that she was the manager of one of his subsidiaries in France. He had a permanent smile, little bitty eyes and wanted to learn all the curse words first.
"Bad words are important, you know" he told me with his German accent.

The first day he arrived at the language school, he stretched his very long arm to shake my hand. I shook his hand; the hand was enormous and strong as a butcher, which I later found out he was before finishing college. He crushed my hand.

"A strong handshake is very important" he said, "and people will remember you".

"Yea" I thought while I nodded, eyes wide, "But not from Big Foot" I thought but stayed quiet. He smiled his corky smile and crossed his eyes at me.

"My name is Christian Hoffman. I am here to learn English" he said.

He was my favorite student. I saw him almost every day in or out of the class room. We went to lunch, to Tijuana and all over San Diego. They both met my girlfriend, my mom, grandmother, the entire family. I had so much fun those few weeks. It was non-stop jokes and laughter. The kind you have with your best friend when you can remember the best times. I smile even now just thinking about it.

Christian, my goofy student, turned out to be the COO of a medium sized software company with offices in Germany, France, Italy, Spain, and all over Europe, all the way down to Istanbul. He was the star of the company with the most sales, the most subsidiaries to manage and the most profitable software installations. To me he just a funny guy with a thick German accent. He didn't want to talk much about business or money, very atypical for the USA. I learned about what he did as an executive more from funny stories he told me about his work than from him explaining the business.

Three days before he left to go back to Germany, he invited me for a cup of coffee.

"Jorge, I want you to work for me" he said. "You can go with me to Germany for two weeks all expenses paid to learn about the country and the company" I was already nodding yes. He continued "If you like what you see, you can come back and pack and move to Germany".

The deal was that one day the company would open a US subsidiary and I could come back to the country someday to work there in the USA. It was a no-brainer. Or so I thought!

Lesson: If You Can Count, Count on Me

How good are you with relationships? Can you make friends easily? Are you the life of the party? Do others consider you the go-to person when they have a problem? There are many ways to measure your relationship success. I like the last one. I like to be the person everyone can count on. Relationships are all about ego. If you think you should be the most important person in the relationship, it will not work. If you're thinking on how this person next to me at a business cocktail party can benefit me, you're not on the right track. Same goes for friendship, marriage, family, work, sales, mentorship and almost every type of relationship.

Greetings from Deutschland

Getting ready for my trip to Germany was fun. I had to buy warm clothes. Living in warm climate only gave me the opportunity to have a thin sweater for every winter. I didn't even own a jacket or a coat. I would receive my two-way ticket to Germany at my PO Box in Chula Vista on L Street, a small city close to the border located in San Diego County. I checked the PO Box two weeks before my trip and the ticket didn't arrive. I checked every day and they weren't there. One day before, I visited the PO Box twice. Once in the afternoon and once before they closed. The ticket didn't arrive. I called Germany and they told me the ticket would be waiting for me at the airport. Oh, what a relief, I was worried there for a moment.

The next day I went to the airport with Gloria (now my wife), my mother, grandmother and my aunt Lissette. We parked the car and we all went inside the airport. No, they didn't just drop me off. Maybe they thought I would get lost on my first international trip. Yes, I'm sure they thought I would get lost.

We entered the San Diego airport earlier than we needed for the flight. I didn't want to miss my flight, or rush, or, well, let's just say I was early to be prepared. I looked at my entourage. They looked nervous.

We all walked to the end of the line at the ticket counter waiting our turn to check in my bag and ask for my ticket. When it was my turn, we all approached the lady at the counter. She typed a few keys. She paused, typed a few more keys and looked and looked up at me from across the counter. "Sorry, there is no ticket waiting for you here. There is no ticket under your name."
I looked back to see everyone. "Could you check under his middle name?" said my aunt, "Sometimes they confused the middle name for a last name". It was a desperate attempt, and it didn't work.
"Sorry, there is no ticket for you anywhere. "Could you please step aside so I can help the next person in line?" she said.

Now I was nervous and my hopes sank alongside my heart. My possible new job, my dream trip to Europe, all gone. I searched for a pay phone.
"I would like to make a collect call to Germany" I told the operator.
"Hoffmann" the deep voice answered on the other side. "Hi Christian, its Jorge" I said.
"Hi Jorge are you at the airport" he asked in his German accent.

He was driving, I could hear the road. Lucky for me he had a car phone. "There is no ticket waiting for me" I said calmly. "I think they must have sent it regular mail and it didn't get here".

I finished explaining that the ticket was not at the airport and nowhere to be found. He thought for a moment. "Alright, buy a ticket and we'll give you the money when you're here". He told me after a short conversation.

"OK" I said voice trembling.

One thousand dollars for a ticket? Oh, my God! That was more money than I had ever seen in my life. I had no money, I had no credit card. I didn't even have a bank account.

"Here, use this" Gloria said while taking out her credit card. She worked at the bank so she had a credit card.

"Do we have thirty days to pay it?" I asked.

"Yes we do" she said, and paid for my ticket. It happened fast, the problem, the shock, and the solution. I was lucky that they parked the car and decided to go in with me. Give one more shout out to lady luck, she's been good to me, give another one to Gloria.

It was a great plane ride and an incredible trip. Christian didn't let me pay for anything. I had one hundred dollars in my pocket and asked:

"Where can I change my money for Deutschmarks?"

"Why do you need them?" he responded.

"In case I want to buy a soda or a something while I go biking around town." I said, feeling uncomfortable without a Deutschmark in my pocket. This was before Euros. "You can't change dollars here." he took out his wallet and handed me a large bill. "For an emergency." he said. Christian and his wife Christiane where incredible hosts and they took me everywhere. I met their friends, their family, even their work colleagues.

After my vacation in Germany, I negotiated a salary and went back home to pack and say my goodbyes. The salary was not what I wanted, especially after taxes in Germany. However I had a company car and a suite at a hotel with kitchen, two bathrooms, and living room. No complaints. I arrived in Germany one month later with my wife, then my girlfriend, eyes wide and filled with hope, and a plan to support my mother and grandmother. I would send half of my net salary to them. With that money, they would fix the leaky roof, get running hot water into the house, pave the road, and pay off the old house. This was my ticket out. I only had to work hard and learn as much as I could. It was the new me, a new adventure. I wasn't nervous. I was excited. How can I be nervous, I had a job, at this stage of my life it's all I ever wanted.

We flew into Dusseldorf and a company employee waited for us. The problem is he drove a Volkswagen Golf and our luggage didn't fit. We packed for a year. We had to make the two-hour trip three times. One to the hotel, back to the airport for more luggage, and back to the little town two hours away. Christian told us to take the week to find our bearings, buy some food at the market and for whatever else we needed. We got in Saturday and could not sleep a wink we were so jetlagged. On Sunday night, we slept at four in the morning. The phone rang at eight AM sharp.

"Why aren't you at work?" an angry voice screamed. "What?" I said half asleep half confused. "It's eight in the morning why aren't you at work?" Christian said. He was mad and he was screaming. I blinked hard to fight the sleep deprivation, searching for an answer, retrieving my memories. "What day is this?" I thought. "Was I supposed to be at work today?" I thought again. I looked around for Gloria. She was still in the bedroom. The phone was all the way in the living room.

"I think you should pack and go back home." He said. "This is not going to work." He continued lowering his voice. "What?" I asked. "You told me to take this week to find the market and report next week. Don't you remember?" I asked gasping for air, or forgiveness, or anything. This was my dream, my goal, the start of my career, the way I would take my family out of poverty. "No" he said. "I don't remember". Tears started to betray me. I choked on my words before they even formed. "This is a misunderstanding." I said. "Ask Korina, she will remember". Korina was a friend and colleague, the one I met in San Diego when I was a teacher only a month or so ago. "Let me speak with her." he said and click, he hung up the phone.

I took a deep breath to bring oxygen back to my brain. I thought for a moment it was a practical joke, a mean, cruel joke. After all he was a funny guy, wasn't he? He was always joking in San Diego. Why was he so mad? After wiping my tears, I went into the bedroom. "What happened?" asked Gloria. I explained everything. "But he told us to take one week." She protested. "I know." I said, maybe it's the translation. Welcome to Germany. This was the beginning of a big, German adventure.

After making a few phone calls I calmed down and got ready for the office as fast as I've ever showered, shaved and dressed. A brisk walk took me there where I sat for two hours in a very large empty office except for a desk and a chair. Gloria came after a couple of hours and I searched rummaged other offices for an extra chair. There we sat looking at each other for the rest of the day. Nothing to do, no computer, no instructions, no manager, nothing. So, it was for a few days until we got laptops and a brief class on the workings of the software. Mind you this was a large software system that takes around a year to learn. I walked around the building that first day. A beautiful and brand new building with an inside garden and a large skylight in the center with surrounding structures making it an attraction for both employees and visitors.

That evening, we left the office at 6 PM and headed for the supermarket to buy food to prepare for dinner. It was closed. To our surprised the supermarket closed daily at 4 PM. Gloria left the office at 5 PM and I left after they kicked me out. "You will be the first one in and the last one out" Christian had told me. I often stayed until the lights went off, I was forced to leave or found myself stuck in the dark far away from the exit.

Soon we decided we had to leave the office earlier one day per week in order to buy our provisions, and so we did for the first time, arriving at the supermarket shortly before it closed. "I'll get a cart" I told Gloria as I walked towards a line of carts parked next to the supermarket. To my surprised they were locked with chains with no way of grabbing one. "This is strange" I told her. "Maybe they're getting ready to close" she remarked back. "We better hurry" I exclaimed. And so, we both walked at a brisk pace towards the entrance of the supermarket. Gloria saw an empty shopping cart standing there waiting for us. When she fetched it and started walking towards the door, a German lady dressed in casual wool clothes and a scarf started screaming at her. We did not understand a word she said, but we quickly realized it was her cart. "How Rude!" I thought. It's just a cart and we did not know it was hers. We soon realized that she was taking the shopping cart back to the proper place with all the other carts to push in the chain and secure her deutschmark. Who would have known? Turns out you need to deposit a coin in order to take a shopping cart out of its cue. Once you bring it back you retrieve your coin. Live and learn.

After she shook off the lady's screams, we hurried up to do our shopping. We know we had only fifteen minutes and the store was all but empty. "You go get the milk and I'll get some tomatoes for our pasta sauce" Gloria told me. As I walked towards the back of the small supermarket looking for milk an employee, a middle-aged lady in her apron grabbed me by the arm and pulled me pointing towards the exit. I gather she was telling me they were closing. "Talk about customer service" I thought. I smiled and yanked my arm nodding yes. No sense to argue in German! "Milch" I told the lady hoping my accent was understandable. She smiled back and nodded.

Not three steps did I take when the lights went out one by one from front to back with a dramatic sound each time one of the industrial size bulbs turned to darkness. As the last of the lights went off and I found myself stuck in a hallway in total darkness I heard a slim voice in the far with a tentative yell of "Jorgeeeee". I knew then, Gloria had turned off the lights by mistake. I was already laughing.

After my eyes adjusted I took a few long and quick steps to make it to the vegetable island, a small department in the front of the store with only a few vegetables. I looked around and saw a light switch on top of the scale used to weigh the produces and I flicked it on. All the lights went

155

on again. "I thought I was turning on the scale" she protested even before I said anything. I laughed. Every day was a similar one filled with experiences both fun and frustrating, with culture shock waiting at every corner. Our cheered attitude and playful matter let us escape the supermarket, a police car that stopped us on the freeway, as well as many other small incidents that happened to fall our way. We attracted such situations as an apple to gravity.

We did not see our boss for an entire week. He lived four hours from the office by car and worked from home or from his office in Metz, France. He arrived in his suit and walked in to our empty office. "How is it?" he asked in a funny cheery voice while inspecting the office lacking of everything but our desk and chairs. "Good." we both said, standing up to take his overly bearing handshake. "Do you speak German?" he asked. I looked at Gloria and her at me. Then he laughed and told us we would start German lessons within the week in the nearby town of Aachen, a short train ride from our town.

Aachen turned out to be a beautiful German town with the type of town plaza you see in the movies. We took the train to the town for German lessons a few times but after a week or so I decided to spend less time in school and more time working. Now looking back, I don't regret the time I worked, but I do not learning German.

Little changed in the past months if anything, there was nobody to teach us the software, no tasks or milestones to achieve, nothing to measure success or failure. We tried to make a change and go to Spain where we could understand the language and go on location with clients but that wasn't very productive. Yes, we helped with the projects, but we spend all day executing mundane tasks in the software. Nothing that would teach us to install and execute an entire installation by ourselves.

I needed to have another heart to heart with my boss. When Christian came to Spain, Gloria and I sat down with him at a restaurant.
"What's our next step after Spain?" I asked him.
"Next step? You have to learn the software." He said. That's what he always said.
"All right, how much time do we have to learn the software?" I asked.
"Are you learning here? Are you advancing?" He asked me in return without answering my question. Gloria and I looked at each other. I thought about my response. He didn't let me think about it. He looked at Gloria. "Are you happy here?" she had a knot in her throat that prevented words from coming up. "Tell me Gloria, what's going on?" he leaned forward and changed his expression completely. "Are you happy here?" he asked in a fatherly tone.
She shook her head unable to speak. She abruptly stopped a tear from running down her check in an effort not to cry. It was too late.

"It's OK Gloria, have something to drink. We don't have to talk about it now." He said.

I was really surprised. This man could be the toughest boss, the hardest negotiator and then the kindest soul you ever encountered. I really didn't' know what to make of it.

After half an hour of laughing at Christian's jokes and funny faces, he promptly turned back the conversation to business.

"Tell me Gloria" he said. "Why aren't you happy here? Do they treat you well?"

Gloria looked at him with her large eyes that answered for her. He understood.

"I know you don't want to get anyone in trouble" he said.

"You won't. I'm your friend and I just want to know what's happening" he said.

"I think they see us as a threat and they're just reacting to a threat" she said.

"No" he said firmly. "You don't have to protect them. There's no excuse for treating you badly. You have to be happy" he smiled. He then turned to me. "Why didn't you tell me this was happening?" he frowned at me but not in a frightening way.

"I just want to work" I said. "I don't care if they ignore me, if they're rude to me, if they treat me badly. That will not stop me. I don't want to give you excuses, just results". I knew this was a lifetime opportunity and I didn't want to lose it because I couldn't' take a little heat form co-workers.

Christian listened patiently. As an old soul. Now as I remember he was younger than I am today, but still seemed so much wiser.

"You go back to Germany now." he said, and that was that. "You are not here to suffer. You are here to learn. But you also need to be happy. If you're not happy, you don't stay. Jorge, Gloria, you will always be happy working with me." he said making a goofy face.

Christian gave me the opportunity to go back to the USA to open a subsidiary and quickly became the CEO of US operations at twenty-eight years old. From there, I maintained executive positions at several companies before starting my own. Years later, after we both left the company, we still had a special friendship. He visited Gloria and me in San Diego and we visited him in Germany. One day as we were spread across his living room, he surprised me again.

"Jorge, you know you changed my life." he said.

I looked at him and looked at Gloria waiting for the punchline. No punchline.

"Yes, you showed me that life is more than work; that life is about family and friends. You showed me how to slow down and see where I am." I smiled slightly. Here was my mentor telling me he learned something from me. I was so proud.

After Christian died, I've been carrying a small hole in my stomach. We postponed our last trip to Germany to see him because of money. Sure, we had money, we just thought we didn't have a lot of it. I also never spoke with his mother and father. "They don't speak English." I've always told myself. They still have all his belongings in his old childhood room. They refuse to give away anything as if he'll be back tomorrow. I will wrap and send a copy of this book to them and call them. Get on a plane if I can. I will tell them how their son still lives every day in the heart of so many people they never even met but he influenced. I will tell his mother how every now and then, when I'm in real need or trouble, I can see him out of the corner of my eye.

Board of Directors

Let me start by telling you it may seem weird, well, let me rethink that. After all, I just told you about my conversations with a Guardian Angel. So, you already think it's weird. Let me try that again. I speak with dead people. No, that's also weird. How about this: I've had more than my fair share of death in my family. Only a few died at their proper age, if there is such thing. My grandmother died in her eighties and she went kicking and screaming. The others died as teenagers and young adults. My Guardian Angel died in his early forties, my two uncles in their twenties, my cousin in his teens, my aunt died, my other uncle, my friend was murdered with his eight-year-old son. Let's just say I've had my share of tragedies.

I've always been concerned with life after death. Not for what will happen to me, but what happened to the ones I love. Are they happy? Are they doing what they like? Did they find the rest of our family and are now in a forever state of euphoria? Do they have new experiences and tell each other stories about those experiences?

When you're born into an extended family, cultures such as the Mexican one, you weave your relationships tightly and often. As often as every day. You talk every day, eat together, share stories, problems and ask for advice from everyone, especially if they're older than you. You grow used to them, to their advice, and your life can't stop when they're gone. You have to have those conversations, ask for guidance. When my friends and family members die, I continue asking them for advice. I figured now their dead they probably know the secrets of the universe and can help me in my mundane problems. This is why I formed a Board of Directors. You're not invited. If you are on the board, you're dead.

The Board of Directors consists of several of my dead friends and family members; people very close to me. People that I shared ideas, dreams, fears and everyday problems. It's not easy to stop a conversation with someone you love and trust completely. You're used to calling them on the phone after something funny happens to you, after a big game or a promotion. Or when life paints you blue and you need a pep talk or just an old fashion kick in the butt. That's why you need a board of directors. To guide you, advise you, be there for you and yes, for the butt kicking that we all need once in a while. There is no reason why you should stop asking the same people for advice after they're gone. After all, what does "gone" really mean? It depends on your beliefs, religion or the lack of it.

I lived with my grandmother and my mother since I was born. Even after I got married I visited my grandmother almost every day. She lived with my aunt only five minutes away from my house. We had coffee together in the morning, after lunch or if I couldn't make it throughout the day, in the evening after work. My aunt was there, my mother and one or two of my cousins. My grandmother asked me about my day, about my friends and other grandchildren that did not visit her as often. I felt peaceful when visiting my grandmother, a sense of accomplishment and of belonging. Coffee is a very important to me and to my family. It's not the caffeine infused beverage that we're after. It's the conversation. Smelling the hot cup of coffee, boiling the milk, sitting and chatting as a family while sharing your most private life experiences. There are no secrets around the kitchen table during coffee.

When I lived in Tijuana, my grandmother used to boil the milk for our coffee in a small pot. She boiled water in another pot and brewed coffee manually by holding an old fashion fabric filter strapped around a wire handle in one hand and pouring the boiling water with the other. We drank a local coffee brand toasted only a few blocks from my house but brought from Veracruz, Mexico. She didn't use a coffee maker until she was much older but still boiled the milk on the gas stove. I sat and looked at her filtering the coffee. Even as a teenager, it was an opportunity to sit and talk with my grandmother.

I saw my grandmother get old over many cups of coffee. Her arthritis slowly deforming her hands, her osteoporosis dissolving her bones, her heart needing replacement parts twice in her life. For thirty years, we shared our coffee almost every day. It was as sure as waking up. Until one day, she didn't. Yes, she lived a long life, loved more than eighty years. But it's not easy stopping a thirty-year-old habit. Whether it's a good habit or a bad one. It's not easy drinking coffee by yourself. So, I don't. I drink coffee with my grandmother, one of my board members. And over one or several cups we chat about the day, about life, about her other grandchildren and greatgrandchildren. I tell her about my problems at work and about the funny thing that happened to me the other day. "Would you care for more coffee?" I asked. "Just half a cup" she used to answer every time.

Like my grandmother, every member of my board of directors is special. Not just as an entity, but special for me.

Ramon had the eyes of a child and he moved at one and a half speed, as a child on sugar would. He walked fast, talked fast, and worked fast. I met him soon after I started a business partnership in wholesale distribution. He worked in the warehouse and quickly became the warehouse manager in his twenties. He only spoke Spanish and lived in Tijuana, crossing the border daily at four or five in the morning to get to work at seven.

Ramon could sort product, jump off the forklift and move pallets and then jumped back down to load a truck all on one cup of coffee and while telling you a dirty joke. He always nodded when he saw you, even if he saw you twenty times per day. He acknowledged you when he saw you or anybody else. The truck driver, the mail woman, neighbors, cleaning crew, everyone, not just his bosses. I'm not sure if it was on purpose or just part of his personality, but every time he did it you felt you were there, you felt part of his world, part of the team, important. He always accompanied his nod with a smile. His smile was frozen in place except when he was concentrating on the computer. He learned how to use the computer because he had to for work. That was the only time he lost his smile, replaced by a concentrated stare.

Several times per month, Ramon had to sleep in his car to start working the next day at four in the morning. He worked the entire day, took a break to eat, and then worked all night until he was exhausted, then he slept on his car and did it again. "I have too much work." he said, "I had to stay in the car to avoid the drive and get the purchase orders out." That should tell you the type of man he was.

He got his father, mother, brother, sister and aunt jobs at the warehouse. They could not keep up with him but it made him happy to have them around, so my partner hired them all to keep him happy. I remember when his first son was born. I remember his son's first birthday party. He was so happy. My wife and I attended. I think I made him feel important that day. He showered us with attention as did his entire family. I bet he didn't know he made me feel important every day.

One day I got the call. The type of phone call that changes your day, your month, your life. My cousin Victor called me. Him and Ramon were best of friends and still worked together after I left the business. It's the call you don't want to get. I went to the funeral. I did it for his family, I did it for me, and I did it for Ramon. I hate funerals. It was a case of mistaken identity and he and his family were sprayed with bullets while driving to the park. He died, his young son died. His wife got hit on the foot and lost it. She lived and so did their young baby.

He was young, too young to die. One of the good guys, one of the examples that you point at and say "look, we should be more like him". So, he's now part of my board, giving me a hard time and slapping me hard on the back with his strong, heavy hands.

Lesson: Your New Board

Try assembling your very own board of directors. Test how it feels, how you feel. Think of a member on your new board and tell them about your day, ask them a question, or share a funny moment from your day. In a world that could make you feel alone, sometimes having an everlasting friend in your corner can help you when you need it.

Think of that person when your mind is quiet. Close your eyes, remember their smile and laughter. What made them happy? How can you make them proud? What advice would they give you if they could give it to you now?

PART III: MORE LESSONS FROM MY GUARDIAN ANGEL

The lessons from my Guardian Angel are implicit in the stories. However, I have some "extra" lessons that I've learned from my guardian angel and would like to share with you.

Look three times before you cross

I was five when my mother taught me to cross the street. "You look three time before you cross", she said in her mentoring tone. "One to the left, one to the right, another to the left, and then you cross". It might not be important when you're fifteen years old. But when you're five or six and have to cross streets daily, it will save your life. I imagine my Guardian Angel always holding my shoulder from behind, a giant figure putting a large hand on a tiny child and counting to three, then letting me go before the next car wizzes by.

Writing stories from your past makes you relive previous days, sometimes it feels like previous lives. That in itself is joyful. However, in writing the stories of this book, I meditated on the people in the stories, both the ones alive and the ones not. On my relationship with them, again, both with the living and the not. With the not living, I close my eyes and see in my mind's eye conversations we had during parties, over coffee, at work or even laughing while drinking a beer. What happens when you vividly remember or relive conversations with the dead? You're remembering now what happened before, but in your mind it's happening now. I know what happens, you feel as if they are here. You feel the love you felt, you smile when you remember their jokes and cry when you open your eyes.

Reading changes you. Not just metaphorically or in intelligence, but it changes you physically. It can change you on the outside, for it surely changes you on the inside, creating semi-permanent and permanent neurological connections that make you smarter. Writing also changes you. You see, sometimes you tell a story but many times a story tells you. In the case of many of the stories in this book, I felt like the speaker for the dead, a reference to the sequel to the book Ender's Game by Orson Scott Card. At the end of the stories I felt the satisfaction of a thirty-year-old friendship, but the regret of not giving more. At the end of the story, I received much more than what I gave. All those in my stories became Guardian Angels. I'm not sure if by coincidence or by choice. But they did.

At the beginning of the story I believed everyone should look for their Guardian Angel, now I believe we should strive to be a Guardian Angel.

Your handshake is your letter of introduction

I know the motions of a hand shake. I've done it hundreds, maybe thousands of times. You stretch you hand out in salutation and after you make contact you close it for a second. Maybe you shake it once up and down if you're feeling bold. "That's not a handshake" said Christian Hoffmann. "That's a sign of a weak personality" He told me. I wasn't amused. My ego got the best of me for the first three seconds. I thought about it another two seconds and let my ego go. "Show me" I said with humility. He reached out his gigantic hand dangling from his unusually long arm. Paying special attention to his posture. Standing straight and tall to appear larger than in reality. I did the same and stretched my hand in salute. He looked me straight in the eyes with a serious gaze and squeezed my hand as if I was a walnut that needed to be cracked. My eyes widen just a little bit and I understood immediately the power of that salutation.

I've had many double takes after people shake my hand since then. Many others asking, "What's your name again?" after a casual uninterested introduction. The handshake lets people know you care about them and I'm here to be noticed, all in the same breath. You should see how my wife fares in her introductions. As small woman weighing roughly one hundred twelve pounds she'll sink her fragile hands into a large man's knuckles making it impossible to see over her head. They will look at me after shaking her hand and "Wow!" will come out of their mouth.

Lesson in Work Ethic

Coming from a working family, work ethic was always embedded in me. Taking pride in your work as well as performing well to honor your family, friends and employer. I saw my mother and grandmother work all day seven days per week. When my mother had some free time, she spent it studying or with me. It was work, work, work! However, that type of hard work is not enough to achieve your goals if you have goals that need to evolve beyond a middle management job. I had to learn from my mentor and now Guardian Angel how to work hard towards the right goal.

Work Ethic is very subjective. It depends on your culture, the type of job, and geographical location. I've had the pleasure and blessing to work with people from Japan, Korea, Germany, the United States, Mexico, Argentina, Spain, UK, France, Belgium and Holland. Working most of my life in the USA, I've worked with people from all over the country. Germans and Japanese are the most impressive in my eyes. They work differently and have a very distinct way of looking at their work. Japan seems to have a very strict code of conduct and hierarchy of power. They work long hours and they are proud of their work. They want to do a good job because of honor. That carries a level of respect that is embedded into the culture. From them I learned to put my name into everything I do. From when I was an entry level employee to now, I make sure everyone knows any document that comes out of my desk is from me. With this comes a level of responsibility to protect the brand, the name, the reputation. Your honor is at stake. If you're going to send that document that says "Created by Your Name" it better be a great looking presentation, letter, or article. You never know who will look at your work. It can end up in the desk of the CEO, a customer, or the president.

In Germany, I learned to be the first person in and the last person out. "Outperform everyone in everything you do". I already knew that lesson from sports. Not being the fastest, tallest or strongest, I always had to out practice everyone to make it to the team. It was easy to understand and apply the analogy. "I'm not afraid of work" I told my boss time and time again. Working alone will take you a long way, but not all the way. Work produces experience but not necessarily the right experience, but the same experience. You become an expert in what you're doing, not in what you want to do. In this case, I wanted to be Vice President and then CEO of a company. How do you practice for that? In my case, you absorb all you can in practice and you read and study like a PhD candidate. When the opportunity comes your way, you'll be prepared with some practice, little experience but a lot of information in your brain from studying and reading. Just like I was sure nobody would outwork me, I was also confident nobody would out study me.

One important note. Working hard doesn't just mean working long hours or weekends. It means growth, income, and sales. If you're not producing income it will be hard to show your work. Many times, I see employees ask for a raise stating they work very hard, but when you ask if they know what impact they have on the bottom line they have no idea of what you're talking about. I took a different strategy. I found out that by producing sales for my first employer I would be rewarded exponentially. So, I changed from consulting to sales immediately and was compensated in the same way.

Lesson in Keeping Friends

As I learned more and more about Christian's relationships in Germany as well as all over the world, I started noticing a pattern. Everyone was wonderful! How can this be? How can you attract such great friends and wonderful employees time after time, all the time? This is not a coincidence.

Christian didn't look for a particular type of friend or employee. He reached out to everyone and waited to see what came back. When the same thing he put out came back, he had a new friend. This is what happened with Gloria and myself and the same happened with all of his friends and co-workers.

Now to the untrained eye this sounds logical, easy and a no-brainer. It's not. Especially as it comes to hiring. Finding talented people that work well together is a bonus in business. The lesson is not in the hiring. It's not even in attracting the right people, although that's a lesson by itself. But for now what I want to focus on is the longevity of the relationship. Let's ask ourselves some questions. How many family members do you have? How often do you speak with them? How about friends that you've made since high school or even before? How many times do you call them on the phone? When you travel and you chat with a stranger at the airport, do you stay in touch? What if I told you my mentor called everyone at least once per month.

That would take hundreds of calls, right? Well, that's what he did. We mere mortals can't be expected to turn into telemarketers making twenty to thirty calls per day just to say hello. But that's what it takes to make people feel important. So, stop reading or listening to this book and go call your mother, sister, friend or somebody important.

Major Lesson: Be a Guardian Angel

The entire set up of the human world is based on survival. To survive, we needed to outsmart, out run or out hide predators, all the while, out maneuver competitors for the same food sources. Imagine a group of early humans walking through long patches of plains, grass knee high as far as the eye can see, with a few trees spread here and there. An entire family of Homo sapiens walking, more like a clan. You have several children in the group as well as adults of different ages. Their survival is entirely tied to the survival of the group. As the world stood for thousands of years, interdependency was the main law of survival.

The world was not a place for individuals. You could not hunt on your own. You could not fight away predators or gather food all while procreating and taking care of the new generation. There was no place for individualism in survival land. Relationships were very close within a clan or tribe. You had to know everyone and understand their role in the group in order to belong, help, and get help from them. If you wanted to go and wonder by yourself without a group, you could last a day, maybe more, but it was a death sentence for you and for the species. If everyone decided to be an individual, it would mean the end of Homo sapiens on planet earth.

As time passed in decades and then centuries, technology evolved to make it possible for groups to become smaller. Farming allowed the relative safety of a small piece of land with a dwelling to protect inhabitants from predators and the elements. You needed a large family to survive, but not a tribe. And so it was that a few scattered homes were not so scattered anymore and new forms of survival sprawled out such as commerce and services, to form small towns and then cities. You know the story, it's your own story, the one from your great-grandfather or his great-grandfather. The industrial revolution launched us into a brand-new world, one where you didn't need to farm to survive, and a new form of work outside the farm was born. So did a form of schooling, teaching young minds how to work as a group not to survive but to sit in a line and build machines, or clothes or consumables.

Now your ancestors are out of the plains, working as large groups. They are out of the farm working as smaller groups and they are in a factory where there is no danger from a tiger or a snake. Where they don't need to rely on the group to survive but on their skills with a hammer, or with a printer, or a piece of machinery that cuts parts for products.

Now you're measured on how much you can produce on your own, without working on a group.

At the same time, we're trained on working by ourselves. Our schools are teaching us to work individually. You get a test that you and only you can answer, collaborating with your friend, neighbor or tribe is not only bad, it's illegal, immoral, and you'll be thrown out of school for cheating. Rules are no longer for collaboration, for working as a team and ensuring the survival of the tribe. They don't measure your capacity to interact with others or help them, to achieve a goal with your team or even to survive in the tribe. This trend sponsors individualism at best, and antisocial behavior at worst. Wining, making money as an individual triumph over having a group win or making money for the family, community or tribe. There are exceptions, such as a team headed by a good coach, where winning as a team trumps scoring points or being a VIP. Where the older players are responsible for the younger players. These exceptions go a long way in life and in the job place, where many companies look to potential employees that played team sports because they know how to work as a team and put the goals of the group before their individual ones.

This bring us to the Guardian Angel profile. If an individual only thinks of their personal needs, it's difficult for them to apply for this responsibility. It takes a very special personality to be a guardian angel. You have to share your candy with other kids!

My eight-year-old godson was sat down to the table to eat in one of our family reunions. He was the first on the table and started eating before everyone. He finished a small piece of meat his grandmother served before he ate the rest of the items on his small plate. His grandmother asked "Would you like another piece of meat?" He chewed and swallow his food, "No thank you" he said. "Yes," grandmother said, "I just gave you a very small piece while I finished the rest, it wasn't enough". "Is there enough for everyone?" he asked his grandmother worried. "Yes, there's plenty and more" said grandmother serving him another piece of meat.

The same small boy paid me a visit house last month with a piece of candy for me. My wife picked him up at school. "He's got candy for you." said my wife. We stopped at the store to buy a treat and he choose a chocolate for you. "My Nino likes chocolate, let's take him some." he had said. He's personality has always been of service. Even when he was four years old. This is the personality we need to have, feed it and harness it to grow up to be a guardian angel.

In other cultures and religions, including Buddhism and Hinduism, the type of higher being is not achieved in just one lifetime. You need meditation, study and experience over multiple lifetimes to learn what's important in life.

You evolve over centuries to reach enlightenment. A state where you understand your place in your home, your world, or the universe.

Let's meditate on this for a moment. According to this believe system an "old soul" is not just an expression. It's a soul that was born, loved, lived, learned and then died. After this it happen again and again until the experience stacked like someone nine hundred years old. How would that person be? What would you see when you look into those eyes? That's an old soul.

I would like to believe that a Guardian Angel is an old soul. The oldest soul. One who lived fifty lives and experienced thousands of years. After all the knowledge and culture, all the living and dying, the praying and the wondering, they concluded that the highest level of happiness is in being a Guardian Angel.

Lessons From My Guardian Angel

Lessons From My Guardian Angel

Continue With Your Guardian Angel Experience...

I would love to hear from you, your experiences, and your stories.

www.LessonsFromMyGuardianAngel.com

Please go to the Guardian Angel website and share your anecdotes with other readers, read more stories and download free podcasts and other fun free material.

Can't wait to hear from you!

Thanks for reading and for sharing.

Jorge S. Olson

www.ingramcontent.com/pod-product-compliance
Lightning Source LLC
Chambersburg PA
CBHW072005090426
42740CB00011B/2103